Master Introductory Psychology

Volume 2

Learning

Memory

Language & Cognition

States of Consciousness

by Michael Corayer

Text, illustrations, and cover design by Michael Corayer

Copyright © 2016 Michael Corayer

Psych Exam Review Press

ISBN 978-0-9970053-0-1

www.psychexamreview.com

Preface

This book is designed to bridge the gap I see between textbooks and study guides. Generally textbooks are overwhelming, as authors attempt to pack in more information than any one student could manage to remember. On the other hand, many study guides are nothing more than glorified term lists, with simple definitions and multiple choice questions that never really get to the heart of psychology. So while there is a great deal of factual information in these pages, the emphasis is on why concepts matter and why certain studies and theories are important. Your approach to using this book should be similar: focus on the purpose and meaning of the information, rather than obsessively studying the terms and definitions. Once you understand the underlying concepts and the practical applications of these ideas, you'll find it easier to remember the terminology.

A Note about Images

As you'll notice, this book is a bit different from other textbooks and study guides in that it is heavy on text and light on images, charts, and boxes. You'll find a few simple images. Are they amazingly detailed and visually stunning? Certainly not. Are some of them so bad that they just might stick in your head and help you remember the material? I hope so. I've focused on simple drawings I could actually draw on the board in a classroom, rather than trying to find (and license) the "perfect" image. Consider that your average textbook licenses hundreds of images, cartoons, and diagrams (thus inflating the price) that a Google search can instantly reveal to you for free. If you want to see Hermann von Helmholtz or what scanning-electron-microscope images of your stereocilia look like, I'm sure you're resourceful enough to find out. Don't just stick to one confusing textbook diagram when you can find thousands of stunning images in a matter of moments.

If you want a little guidance in tracking down the images that help bring psychology to life, you can start by checking out my Pinterest boards at **www.pinterest.com/psychexamreview** for hundreds of images (as well as articles and videos) on psychology, all organized by topic. For even more resources, check out **www.psychexamreview.com**

Table of Contents

Chapter 1
Learning

Learning

On a common-sense level we all know what learning is, but how can we come up with a precise definition of learning? How can we measure learning? As a teacher, I wonder every day whether my students have learned something because I can't really get inside their heads to find out. In school situations, we generally depend on observation to determine whether learning has occurred. We don't just take your word that you've learned something, we want to see evidence. This is actually very similar to how behavioral psychologists of the 1920s to 1950s thought about learning. They believed that the inner workings of the mind weren't important; what mattered was observable behavior. With this emphasis on behavior, we can say that *learning* is a relatively long-lasting change in behavior that results from our experience with the world. Because of this emphasis on behavior in assessing learning, the conditioning theories we'll learn about in this chapter are often collectively referred to as *behaviorism*. Behavior is not the only way of assessing learning, and as we'll see at the end of this chapter, research eventually moved away from a strict emphasis on behavior. But before we get ahead of ourselves, let's look to the start of behaviorist psychology with the work of Ivan Pavlov.

Classical Conditioning

Chances are you've heard someone mention "Pavlov's dog" or something being a "Pavlovian response", so let's take a look at the details of some of Pavlov's work and the key terms for discussing what is known as *classical conditioning*.

Ivan Pavlov was a Russian physiologist studying digestion in dogs (for which he won the Nobel prize in 1904) who noticed an interesting phenomenon. Pavlov had been collecting saliva samples from dogs when food was presented to them, but he noticed that the dogs began salivating even before the food was presented (like while the researcher was preparing the food). It was as if the dogs knew that food was on the way.

Pavlov then wanted to see if dogs could also learn to expect food (shown by their salivation) following a particular stimulus like a bell, a metronome, a light, etc. In the most well-known version of his experiments, he rang a bell prior to the presentation of food. Initially the bell was a meaningless sound, but by repeatedly following that sound with food, Pavlov was able to teach the dogs to salivate whenever the bell rang.

In this case, the bell started as a *neutral stimulus* (*NS*), meaning that it didn't elicit a response on its own. If you go up to a random dog on the street and ring a bell, there isn't a specific response that will occur. The food, however, would be an *unconditioned stimulus* (*US*), because it doesn't need to be conditioned, or taught to the dog. If you give food to any random dog, a predictable response will occur: salivation. This response, salivating to food, hasn't been taught so it's called an *unconditioned response* (*UR*). Conditioning consists of repeatedly presenting the neutral stimulus followed by the unconditioned stimulus, which will automatically cause the unconditioned response.

After enough training, the neutral stimulus will be able to elicit a predictable response all by itself. The previously neutral stimulus can now be called a *conditioned stimulus* (*CS*). The response that has been taught, salivating to the sound of a bell, is now called a *conditioned response* (*CR*). When the dog has learned to salivate to the sound of the bell, we can say that *acquisition* has occurred. Here's a summary of the steps in classical conditioning:

Before Conditioning

Neutral Stimulus (bell) alone **:** no response

Unconditioned Stimulus (food) alone **:** Unconditioned Response (salivate)

The Conditioning Process

Neutral Stimulus (bell) then Unconditioned Stimulus (food)**:** Unconditioned Response (salivate)

After repeating this several times, the Neutral Stimulus becomes a Conditioned Stimulus, which means...

After Conditioning

Conditioned Stimulus (bell)**:** Conditioned Response (salivate to the bell)

If we stop pairing the bell with food, this conditioned response won't continue on forever. Eventually, the dog will stop responding to the stimulus, and we can say that **extinction** has occurred. But just because the dog has stopped responding to the stimulus doesn't necessarily mean that the dog has completely forgotten the learning. In fact, Pavlov found that after extinction the conditioned response would reappear after a rest period of about a day. This was referred to as **spontaneous recovery** and shows us that the dog hasn't forgotten the association, he has just temporarily stopped responding. In addition, if this dog were to be trained with bell/food pairings again in the future, he would relearn the association more quickly than a dog without any prior conditioning.

After teaching the dogs to salivate to the sound of a bell, Pavlov found that they also salivated to the sound of a similar bell (playing a slightly different tone). This became known as **stimulus generalization**. After conditioning, the conditioned response can occur in the presence of stimuli which are similar to the conditioned stimulus. As an interesting side note, Pavlov found that the response to other tones weakened as the tone frequencies got farther and farther from the original stimulus, but then increased when reaching an octave, indicating that dogs also perceive octaves as sounding like the "same" note just as we do.

With more conditioning, Pavlov discovered that he could teach the dogs to respond only to a particular stimulus. For example, by always presenting the food in the presence of a particular tone but never in the presence of a second (different) tone, Pavlov could eventually condition the dogs to only salivate to the first tone. This ability to differentiate two similar stimuli is known as **stimulus discrimination.**

Pavlov also found that after dogs had been conditioned to salivate to a bell, he could get them to salivate to a light by turning it on before the bell, even though the light was never directly paired with food. This is known as **second-order conditioning** or **higher-order conditioning**. Because the dogs had learned that the bell meant food was coming, then learned that the light meant that the bell was coming, they would salivate to the light.

Pavlov wasn't the only one conducting experiments in classical conditioning. ***John B. Watson*** and ***Rosalie Rayner*** conducted a study in 1920 showing that classical conditioning could be used to teach fear. In an ethically-questionable procedure, Watson and Rayner presented a white rat to an 8-month old baby (known as "Little Albert"), then hit a metal bar with a hammer, creating a loud, startling noise which made Albert cry. After repeated pairings of the rat with the loud noise, they found that Albert would show distress when the rat was presented, suggesting that fears could develop via classical conditioning, known as ***aversive conditioning***. Albert also showed ***stimulus generalization*** because he showed distress not only to rats, but also to other furry objects like a rabbit and a white-bearded mask that Watson wore.

Biological Aspects of Conditioning

There are biological constraints on which types of associations can be learned via classical conditioning. While studying the effects of radiation on rats, John Garcia and colleagues noticed that the rats refused to drink water from the dishes in their cages following radiation exposure. The radiation was making the rats sick, and apparently the rats were automatically associating this illness with the water they had drank prior to exposure. This suggested that the rats had a biological predisposition to learn relationships between food and illness. Garcia and Robert Koelling conducted later studies teaching rats to associate a noise with an electric shock which followed and to associate flavored water with subsequent nausea, but they discovered that they couldn't teach rats to associate noise with nausea or drinking flavored water with an electric shock. This demonstrates that we have a ***biological preparedness*** for certain types of learning and some pairings will be learned more easily than others. If we consider an evolutionary approach to understanding this, it makes sense that we should be able to quickly learn to associate illness with food (so we can avoid that food in the future) while associating nausea with noise would be less practical. This ***learned taste aversion*** doesn't quite follow the rules of classical conditioning because there may only be a single pairing of a food with illness as well as a long delay between the two, and yet the learning can still occur.

If you've seen Stanley Kubrick's *A Clockwork Orange* (based on the novel by Anthony Burgess), you might recall the scene in which Alex is taught to avoid violence via classical conditioning. He's given an injection that makes him feel sick (though he was told it was a vitamin supplement) and is then forced to watch violent films. The goal is for him to be conditioned to associate violence with illness, thus avoiding violence in the future. While it may sound like a good idea in theory, in practice Alex would have a biological predisposition to associate his illness with whatever food had been served to him hours earlier and not with the violent films he was forced to watch.

Operant Conditioning

Though classical conditioning provided some explanation for the formation of associations between stimuli and automatic responses, it didn't provide much insight on the development of voluntary behaviors. In studies of classical conditioning, the organism being studied is rather passive. Pavlov's dogs simply stood around waiting for bells to ring, food to be presented, etc. They weren't exploring the environment, searching for food, or interacting with stimuli. In order to understand these real-life behaviors, we need to look to another type of conditioning, in which the organism operates on the environment and experiences the consequences of its behavior.

To begin, we'll look to one of the first researchers in this area, ***Edward Thorndike***. Thorndike placed a hungry cat in a box, then placed food outside the box. Inside the box was a lever which, when pressed, would cause the door to open, allowing the cat access to the food dish. Thorndike would repeatedly place cats in this "puzzle box", and observe how long they took to escape. Thorndike found that the cats learned that pressing the lever opened the door and they became successively faster with each trial. Initially they may have stumbled upon the lever accidentally, but after repeated placement in the box, the cats had learned how to escape.

After observing his cats escaping from these puzzle boxes, Thorndike postulated the simple ***Law of Effect***, stating that behavior which is followed by positive consequences is more likely to be repeated. In this case, pressing the lever gave the hungry cats access to food, so this lever pressing would be more likely to be repeated. Thorndike referred to this as ***instrumental learning***: learning to perform behaviors which bring positive consequences.

Thorndike's research examining the relationship between behavior and consequences laid the groundwork for **B.F. Skinner**'s research (if your name was Burrhus Frederic, you'd prefer to go by B.F. as well). Skinner examined behaviors and their outcomes in greater detail, believing that nearly all behaviors could be explained by their associations with rewards or punishments.

Skinner referred to a desirable consequence of a behavior as **reinforcement**, because it reinforced to the animal that this was a behavior that should be repeated in the future. Reinforcement could come in many forms, from things which satisfy basic biological drives like food or warmth (known as **primary reinforcers**), to things like grades, stickers, or money (known as **secondary reinforcers**), which are rewarding due to learned associations (using money to buy food, being praised for good grades, etc.).

Skinner differentiated between **positive reinforcement**, in which an organism receives something desirable (like food), and **negative reinforcement**, in which an organism has something undesirable removed (like turning off electric shocks or loud noises). Imagine you have a terrible headache. You perform the behavior of taking a pill and your headache goes away. This will make it more likely that you'll take a pill in the future (whenever you have a headache) and so the behavior of pill-taking is being reinforced. It's important to note that both types of reinforcement (positive and negative) are used to encourage a behavior so that it will be repeated. This is a commonly-confused concept of conditioning, particularly in popular culture, as films and television shows have often mistakenly referred to negative reinforcement when they should have referred to punishment.

Some consequences reduce the likelihood of a behavior being performed in the future. This is **punishment**. There are also two main types of punishment. **Positive punishment** is receiving something unpleasant. So when you touch a button and receive a painful electric shock, you'll be less likely to touch that button in the future. **Negative punishment** (also known as **omission training**) is when something desirable is taken away as a result of a behavior. So a police officer issuing a fine (taking away money) for speeding is a negative punishment designed to reduce the behavior of speeding in the future.

While punishment can be effective in quickly stopping behavior (like if you press a button and receive a shock), one of the problems it has is that it doesn't provide any information about which behaviors are desirable. In addition, punishments often don't follow immediately after the undesirable behaviors, and therefore may not actually be associated with those behaviors. From the example above, rather than reducing speed, in the future a driver may simply drive on other roads in an attempt to avoid police (associating the fine with getting caught, not with speeding).

The "Skinner Box"

Skinner studied the different effects of reinforcement by placing animals like rats or pigeons inside what he called "***operant boxes***" (often referred to by others as "Skinner boxes") which offered food rewards for behaviors like lever pressing or disc pecking. These boxes tracked how often the animal performed the behavior, and this data could clearly demonstrate increases in behavior based on reinforcement.

Skinner also found that behaviors could be successfully linked together in what is known as ***chaining***. For instance, a pigeon might be reinforced for pushing a lever and also reinforced for pecking a disc, and then these two behaviors could be chained together so the pigeon is only rewarded for pecking the disc and then pressing the lever.

For teaching more complex behaviors, Skinner would reinforce successive approximations of the desired behavior; a process known as ***shaping***. If you want to teach a rat how to play basketball you can't simply wait around for the rat to pick up a ball and place it into a hoop then reinforce this behavior. A behavior this complex won't just suddenly occur on its own (like pecking a disc or pressing a lever might) and therefore it needs to be gradually developed. In this particular case, a rat might first be reinforced just for touching a ball. Then this wouldn't be good enough, and the rat would only be rewarded for actually picking up the ball, then only for carrying it to one side of the cage, then only for placing it inside a basket, and so on until the rat is only rewarded for completing the full behavior (picking up the ball, carrying it to the raised hoop, and dropping the ball in).

This process of shaping applies to human behaviors as well. If we want kids to learn calculus, we don't sit around just waiting for them to solve an integral equation so we can reward them. First we reward counting, then addition, subtraction, multiplication, algebra, etc. until finally we only reward the complex behavior (Mom probably doesn't praise you for adding 3+4 like she used to, now it seems you've got to bring home an A in multivariate calculus to get any rewards).

By closely monitoring the occurrence of behaviors and the frequency of rewards, Skinner was able to look for patterns. Receiving a reward each time the lever is pressed would be an example of **continuous reinforcement**. But Skinner also wanted to know how behavior might change if the reward wasn't always present. This is known as **intermittent reinforcement** (or partial reinforcement). By tracking the accumulated behavioral responses of animals in his operant boxes over time, Skinner could see how different reward schedules influenced the timing and frequency of behavior. Though each of these approaches could be varied in countless ways, there were 4 general types of schedules that Skinner tested.

Schedules of Reinforcement

Fixed-Ratio (The Vending Machine)

A fixed-ratio schedule follows a consistent pattern of reinforcing a certain number of behaviors. This may come in the form of rewarding every behavior (1:1) or only rewarding every 5th response (5:1), according to some set rule. Just as nobody continuously feeds coins to a broken vending machine, when the set ratio is violated (like when each level press no longer delivers food), animals quickly learn to reduce their behavior.

Variable-Ratio (The Slot Machine)

A variable-ratio schedule rewards a particular behavior but does so in an unpredictable fashion. The reinforcement may come after the 1st level press or the 15th, and then may follow immediately with the next press or perhaps not follow for another 10 presses. The unpredictable nature of a variable-ratio schedule can lead to a high frequency of behavior, as the animal (or human) may believe that the next press will "be the one" that delivers the reward.

This is the type of reinforcement seen in gambling, as each next play could provide the big payoff. Skinner found that behaviors rewarded with a variable-ratio schedule were most resistant to extinction. To illustrate this, consider a broken vending machine (fixed ratio) versus a broken slot machine (variable-ratio). How long would you keep putting money into a broken vending machine? You'd probably give up after your first or maybe second try didn't result in a delicious Snickers bar. But now imagine playing a slot machine that is broken and unable to pay out (though everything else appears to be working). You might play 15 times or more before you cease your coin-inserting and button-pressing behavior.

Fixed-Interval (The Paycheck)

In a fixed-interval schedule, reinforcement for a behavior is provided only at fixed time intervals. The reward may be given after 1 minute, every 5 minutes, once an hour, etc. What Skinner found when implementing this schedule was that the frequency of behavior would increase as the time for the reward approached (ensuring that the animal gets the reward), but would then decrease immediately following the reward, as if the animal knew that another reward wouldn't be arriving any time soon.

This may be of concern for human fixed-interval situations like biweekly or monthly paychecks, as work effort may be reduced immediately after a paycheck has been received (just as most students reduce studying effort in the days immediately following exams, because the next exams aren't coming for a while).

Variable-Interval (The Pop-Quiz)

In a variable-interval schedule, reinforcement of a behavior is provided at a varying time interval since the last reinforcement. This means a pigeon might be rewarded for pecking after 10 seconds, or it might be rewarded after 1 minute, then after 5 minutes, then 5 seconds and the time interval between reinforcements is always changing. This schedule produces a slow and steady rate of response. The pigeon pecks steadily so it doesn't miss any opportunities for reinforcement but there's no need to rush, since that won't influence the length of delays.

A human comparison might be a class with pop-quizzes for extra credit given at varying and unpredictable times. These would encourage students to study a little each day to always be prepared to earn some points, though they probably wouldn't cram for hours and hours every night.

Superstitious Minds

Skinner also tried rewarding the animals at random, dropping food into the box at unpredictable times that didn't correspond to any particular desired behavior. Rather than doing nothing and just waiting for the food to arrive, the animals who were rewarded randomly developed bizarre "superstitious" behaviors.

If the animal was lifting a leg or turning his head in the moment preceding the reward, this behavior would be reinforced, making it more likely to be repeated. If, by chance, this behavior was repeated as the reward was delivered again (randomly), this would further serve to reinforce the behavior. As a result, Skinner found pigeons turning in circles or hopping on one leg, simply as a result of this random reinforcement. From this we may view all sorts of superstitious human behaviors, from rain dances to lucky charms to salt thrown over the shoulder, as the result of chance occurrences of reinforcement.

Behavior Reinforcing Behavior

David Premack did research with monkeys which suggested that some behaviors are naturally more desirable than others, and they could therefore be considered to be **high-probability behaviors**. This is known as the *relativity theory of reinforcement* or the **Premack Principle**. In essence it means that we can use preferences for one behavior as reinforcement for another behavior, such as letting a child play video games (presumably a high-probability behavior) only after finishing a number of math problems (presumably a low-probability behavior).

So if your mom ever insisted that you could only play after you finished your homework, now you know she was actually applying this Premack principle, attempting to use a desirable behavior (game playing) to reinforce a less desirable behavior (doing homework). Of course, preferences for some behaviors may vary between individuals, which will influence which behaviors can be used as reinforcement. Some children may love solving math problems and hate playing video games, so our strategy above wouldn't work well for them.

Biological Limits to Learning

Earlier we saw Garcia and Koelling's research on food aversions demonstrating that biological drives influence the associations that can be formed in classical conditioning. Keller and Marian Breland also found that they weren't able to train animals to perform certain tasks which conflicted with biological instincts. For instance, rather than carrying coins to a piggy bank, they found that pigs would repeatedly "root" the coins, pushing them around with their snouts as if the coins were food. Similarly, raccoons would repeatedly rub coins together and attempt to wash them with their paws, something that they usually do with food prior to eating. Both of these demonstrate *instinctual drift*, which is when a behavior being conditioned is similar to an instinctual behavior, and as a result, the instinct takes over and prevents the conditioning from being acquired properly.

Cognitive Learning

The strict focus on observable behavior couldn't last forever and eventually psychologists began considering the cognitive elements of learning more closely. Over time, evidence began to accumulate that we could actually study cognitive elements in a scientific manner, and as a result, psychology shifted away from its emphasis on behavior and started on what is often referred to as the "cognitive revolution". In the following two chapters we'll look at cognition more closely, but before we do so, let's look at some of the theories that shifted the tide away from the behaviorist view and towards a cognitive approach.

Beyond Associations: The Contingency Model of Classical Conditioning

You might wonder, if Pavlov's dogs knew to expect food during his bell experiments, why didn't they always salivate to Pavlov's mere presence? Why weren't they just salivating as soon as he walked into the room and started setting up his bells, lights, and metronomes? There were innumerable things that the dogs could have associated with food (the presence of Pavlov, the dog happening to wag his tail before food arrived, the clock on the wall, the clipboard on the table for Pavlov to record data, etc, etc, etc.). This suggests that while the dogs may have been learning that all of these other stimuli are associated with food, this mere association wasn't enough to cause salivation.

The ***Rescorla-Wagner model*** suggests that a dog in Pavlov's experiment wasn't just learning an association between the bell and the food, but was really learning that the bell is a ***reliable predictor*** of food. Part of the reason the bell is a reliable predictor is because the bell is ***salient***. Pavlov may be standing there the whole time, so the dog may look at him without food arriving, or may not be looking at him just before food arrives, but we can be sure that the bell will at least temporarily capture the dog's attention just before the food. Rescorla and Wagner's contingency model of conditioning emphasizes that we don't just want to learn associations, we want to know what these associations mean and how accurate our predictions about the world will be.

Observational Learning

Imagine that you watch me walk up to a strange device you've never seen before. I press a button and immediately scream out in pain as I receive an electric shock. Are you willing to try pressing the button? Or perhaps I press a different button; a slot opens, and cash pours out into my hands. How likely is it that you would press this button?

According to strict theories of behaviorism, the probability of a behavior should only change when you are reinforced or punished. In this scenario, however, this view doesn't quite work, as you haven't actually been rewarded or punished, and in fact, you haven't really even performed a behavior. Yet we see that your probability of performing a particular behavior has in fact been modified by your experience of watching me. You've learned something about the button-pressing behavior without needing to do it yourself. The idea that we can learn without actually doing led Albert Bandura to investigate whether something like aggressive behavior might be learned simply through observation. To study this, Bandura had children observe an adult playing with a "Bobo doll", a large inflatable toy.

Some of the children saw an adult's behavior that was "aggressive"; punching, kicking, throwing, and beating the doll, while other children were not exposed to this aggressive play (instead the adult quietly played with tinker toys). Bandura wanted to see if observing this behavior had an effect on how the children later played with the toys. After observing the adult, the children were allowed to play with the toys in the room including the Bobo doll. Bandura then observed and recorded the children's actions, looking for mimicry of the behaviors, as well as novel "aggressive" behaviors.

It may not be surprising to learn that Bandura found children directly mimicking behaviors they had observed. Children exposed to the "aggressive" adult play were more likely to perform the "aggressive" behaviors themselves, suggesting that they had learned aggression via what Bandura called ***modeling***.

In later versions of the study, Bandura rewarded (with candy) or punished (via scolding) the adult models, to see if this influenced the children's subsequent behavior. He referred to the consequences the children observed as *vicarious reinforcement*. Bandura found that children could demonstrate the effects of reinforcement (or punishment) on behavior simply by watching another person be rewarded (or punished) for performing that behavior. This has important implications for understanding how children can learn so many behaviors so quickly, as they don't necessarily need to experience all the consequences through trial-and-error in order to learn appropriate behavior.

While it may seem obvious that children learn by observing and mimicking behavior, Bandura's study demonstrated that direct reinforcement wasn't necessary for learning, which also implies that there were cognitive elements at play while children were watching the adult's behavior.

Latent Learning

Edward Tolman conducted research in the 1930s and 40s, though the dominance of a behaviorist approach to understanding learning at that time meant that his work was largely ignored until the 1960s. In one classic study, Tolman and Charles Honzik (1930) divided rats into 3 different conditions and had them complete the same maze repeatedly over the course of 17 days. They monitored each rat and counted the number of errors it made in completing the maze.

For the first group of rats, there was a food reward at the end of the maze. As we would expect from operant conditioning, these rats quickly learned to run to the end of the maze to get their reward, and they gradually made fewer and fewer errors over the course of the 17 days. For the next group of rats, there was no food reward at the end of the maze. Again, without reinforcement, behaviorist theory would suggest that the rats wouldn't learn anything, and not surprisingly, these rats wandered around the maze day after day, and the number of errors they made didn't decrease much over the 17 days.

So far you may be wondering why Tolman's work is still remembered today. As you might guess, the interesting part of the study comes with the third group of rats. This group did not have a food reward at the end of the maze for the first 10 days, then for the last 7 days a food reward was added. A behaviorist might predict that these rats would wander for 10 days, then gradually start learning beginning on the 11th day. But this is not what happened! While these rats did wander aimlessly for the first 10 days, once the food reward was available they rapidly reduced the number of errors they made, and in the last few days these rats actually performed better than the rats in the first group, who had been rewarded all along.

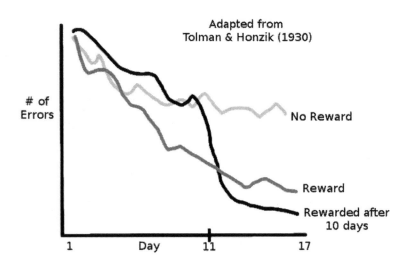

This suggests that the rats in the third group actually were learning during those first 10 days, they just weren't demonstrating their learning yet because there was no incentive to do so. Tolman referred to this as **latent learning**. This is learning that occurs without reinforcement, and isn't demonstrated until there is an incentive or reward.

This type of learning isn't just for rats in mazes, and in fact you probably do it all the time. Teachers rely on the fact that students engage in latent learning during classes and lectures. We assume that between when class started and when class ended you actually learned something, even though we may not have provided any way for you to demonstrate this learning. Just like the rats who waited 10 days before showing how well they knew the maze, you probably have waited weeks in order to demonstrate all the learning leading up to that midterm or final exam.

In another study, Tolman repeatedly placed a rat into a simple maze with only one route available and other routes blocked. The rat would run straight, turn left, then right, then turn right again, then run down a long hallway which ended with a food reward. After learning this maze, the rat was then placed in a similar maze, except the first straight path was blocked and several hallways were available in other directions. A behaviorist would expect the rat to either choose the most similar hall (almost straight) or perhaps to turn left, since that was the first turn it usually made. Instead, the rats showed that they actually knew the general location of the food in relation to the starting point, and correctly turned down the path angling off to the right and leading to the food, even though this angled right turn had never been rewarded in the past. This suggests that the rats had learned a *cognitive map*, a mental representation of the food's location, rather than just the behaviors (i.e. turn left, turn right, turn right) which had been rewarded in the past.

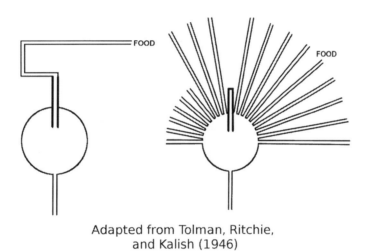

Adapted from Tolman, Ritchie, and Kalish (1946)

Humans also use cognitive maps and this is easily demonstrated if you imagine arriving at a restaurant. While you wait to be seated, you ask to use the restroom and are instructed to walk straight, turn left, turn right, then go to the end of the hallway. Later in the evening, after being seated at your table, you need to use the restroom again. Instead of following the specific previous behaviors (turn left, turn right) you now need to perform new behaviors to get to the restroom (walk straight, turn left) because you are starting from your table. Rather than becoming hopelessly lost and soiling your pants, you use a cognitive map of your position in relation the location of the bathroom to figure out a new route with relatively little effort.

Abstract Learning

We don't only learn specific behaviors tied to specific situations or stimuli. We also learn more complex concepts like what a tree is (we can understand that a willow is a tree and a palm tree is a tree, even though they look quite different). Similarly, we're capable of learning other abstract concepts like love, humility, or pride and these influence our thoughts and behavior even though they may not be readily observable.

While we may excel at it, this ability to learn concepts may not be limited to humans. In fact, research has shown that even pigeons can demonstrate this type of abstract learning. After being taught to peck a picture of a chair, pigeons could also peck at pictures of chairs that they hadn't seen before. While this may seem like just stimulus generalization, their ability to correctly respond to a novel stimulus suggests the possibility that pigeons actually have a cognitive understanding of the concept of chair. In a study by Shigeru Watanabe, Junko Sakamoto, and Masumi Wakita (1995), pigeons were taught to differentiate between Picasso and Monet paintings and later could do so with paintings from these artists they had not seen before. This implies that there are important cognitive elements in their learning process that can't be fully understood through simple behavioral observation.

Insight Learning

Wolfgang Köhler studied learning in chimps and presented them with puzzles to solve in order to obtain bananas. Bananas were suspended high above the ground or placed out of reach behind a fence, and chimps needed to stack boxes to stand on or use sticks to drag the bananas closer. Once the chimps had figured out what to do, they worked at that solution (such as stacking boxes) until they were able to perform it successfully. Köhler observed that the behavior of the chimps differed from that of Thorndike's cats, who discovered the solution to the puzzlebox by simple trial-and-error. It wasn't the case that the chimps simply stumbled onto the solution, but instead that they mentally worked out a solution then acted in a purposeful way.

Rather than a gradual strengthening of a stimulus-response association, the learning in this case seemed to appear in the form of a sudden realization, which Köhler considered to be an example of *insight*. After their initial failures to reach the bananas, the chimps seemed to contemplate solutions, rather than constantly trying new behaviors. This suggests an internal cognitive learning process that is occurring without the need for repeated trial-and-error behavior.

End of an Era

The accumulating evidence of biological and cognitive aspects of learning gradually led to the decline of behaviorism as the dominant approach in psychology. In the following two chapters on memory, language, and cognition, we'll attempt to better understand the internal workings of the mind and how our mental representations of the world influence our thoughts, emotions, and behaviors.

Chapter Summary – Learning

- *Classical conditioning* refers to learning which results from the repeated pairing of stimuli. A neutral stimulus is followed by an unconditioned stimulus (which generates an unconditioned response) repeatedly until the neutral stimulus alone causes a response (called a conditioned response) at which point the neutral stimulus is referred to as a conditioned stimulus.

- In *operant conditioning* an organism learns to associate rewards and punishments with particular behaviors. Positive and negative reinforcement both encourage a behavior either by giving something desirable or taking away something undesirable, while positive and negative punishment discourage a behavior by giving something undesirable or taking away something desirable.

- Reinforcement in operant conditioning can be given according to different schedules including *fixed-ratio*, *variable-ratio*, *fixed-interval*, and *variable-interval*.

- We have *biological predispositions* for some types of learning such as associating taste with nausea. *Instinctual drift* can also prevent some behaviors from being learned properly.

- Increasing evidence for cognitive components of learning from studies of *latent learning*, *observational learning*, *abstract learning*, and *insight learning* eventually led researchers away from a strict emphasis on behavior for understanding learning.

Notes

Chapter 2
Memory

Memory

Why do we remember some things and not others? How much can we remember and how long can our memories last? What processes shape our memory of the world? Memories are a fundamental part of who we are, so it's natural that we should have so many questions about why some memories persist while others fade, or how it is that we can win a game of Trivial Pursuit and on the same night forget where we left our keys.

We can think of the memory process as having three distinct phases: encoding, storage, and retrieval. You'll notice that these words are shared with computer terminology and this is a result of a shift in thinking during the 1950s and 1960s as psychology began to think of the mind as being similar to a computer in how it processes information.

Encoding refers to the process of transforming information into a memory or creating a new memory.

Storage refers to maintaining the memory over time, whether that means holding onto it for a few minutes   or for a lifetime.

Retrieval refers to getting access to a memory that has been stored.

As we'll see throughout this chapter, failures are possible at any of these steps in the memory process. These different types of memory failures will have different characteristics, depending on whether encoding, storage, or retrieval has been affected. We'll also look at how mnemonic techniques can be used to help reduce memory failure and how knowing more about how your memory works can help you to use it more effectively.

Let's begin with a fairly simple model for our different types of memory. The ***3-Box information processing model*** proposed by Richard Atkinson and Richard Shiffrin divides memory into 3 types: sensory memory, short-term memory, and long-term memory. While the latter two types may be familiar to you in everyday use, you may not be familiar with the first type.

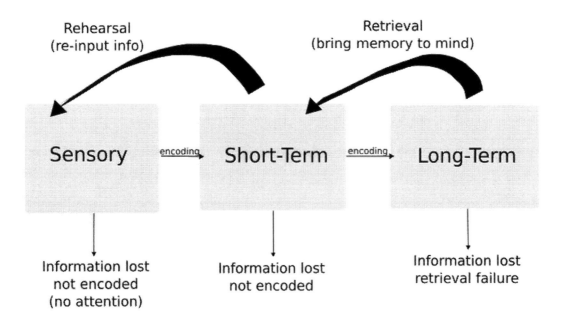

Sensory Memory

Sensory memory is the first "box" in this model. Sensory memory is a highly detailed and accurate representation of information from our senses, which only lasts for about a second. Because it lasts so briefly, it's difficult to study sensory memory, but **George Sperling** devised a clever way to investigate it. Sperling showed participants a slide containing 3 rows of 4 letters (such as below) for only 1/20 of a second.

J   B   W   F

R   W   M   L

N   Q   D   G

He then immediately asked the participants to recite what they saw on either the top, middle, or bottom row. He found that participants were generally able to recall any row he asked for with near perfect accuracy, provided that he asked immediately (errors quickly increased if the delay was 1 second or longer). Participants were essentially "reading" the letters off of a fleeting mental image and this short-lived visual information store is known as *iconic memory* (while auditory sensory memory is referred to as *echoic memory*). This research indicates that the sensory memory store actually contains all of the letters, but that this storage lasts very briefly. Despite their ability to recall **any** row requested, the participants weren't able to recall **all** of the rows. The sensory memory store dissipates so quickly that in the time it took to recite one row, the others had disappeared from memory and could no longer be recalled accurately.

By focusing their attention on one of the rows (the one requested) participants were able to store that information a bit longer. This also demonstrates the role of *selective attention* in memory storage. We can only pay attention to a small amount of the information in our sensory memory at once, and this dictates which information will make its way to the next "box" of the 3-box model: short-term memory.

Short-Term Memory

Research by **George Miller** has estimated that short-term memory can hold somewhere between 5 to 9 items (described in a classic paper titled: *The Magical Number 7 Plus or Minus 2*). When asked to recall a list of words, a string of digits, or a sequence of colors, most people do fine up to about 7 items, after which accuracy drops off sharply. This "**magical number 7**" can be extended through the use of mnemonic techniques such as looking for relationships and patterns among items or creating stories. These techniques are known as **organizational encoding**. One particular type of organizational encoding, known as **chunking**, consists of placing multiple items into groups. For example, if you wanted to remember the number 2317761945007 rather than think of individual digits you might create chunks you recognize such as "Michael Jordan's jersey #", "Declaration of Independence signed", "End of WWII", and "James Bond's agent number" allowing you to recall all 13 digits while only needing to remember 4 items.

Short-term memory only lasts for about 10-30 seconds, but this can be extended by **rehearsal**; mentally repeating the items to keep them from fading. This is essentially a way of re-inputting the information into sensory memory, allowing us to repeat the cycle. If attention is divided or distracted, however, rehearsal will no longer be effective. You may have experienced this if you've ever been interrupted while mentally trying to repeat a phone number. Since Atkinson and Shiffrin first proposed the 3 box model, some changes have been made, including the addition of the term **working memory**. Working memory refers to information in short-term memory that is currently being manipulated. For example, when you are attempting to add several numbers, like solving 478 plus 23, you need to hold each of these numbers in your mind, but you also need to be able to work with them and keep track of changes.

Long-Term Memory

The final memory store in the 3-box model is **long-term memory**. There isn't a known capacity limit for human long-term memory, so there isn't a point at which your memory can be considered "full" and you can no longer encode any new memories. The duration of long-term memory varies greatly; some items may be held for a matter of hours, others for a lifetime.

Long-term memories can be divided into 3 main types: episodic, semantic, and procedural. **Episodic memories** are sequential events and narrative stories that make up your own personal history. These might include memories of your third-grade class, a first date, or a vacation. These are generally remembered as a "gist" of the story and not as a list of specific facts. So when I ask you about your vacation, your episodic memory allows you to give a general description of the overall experience.

Semantic memory consists of factual knowledge of the world; names, dates, word meanings, categories, etc. Both episodic and semantic memories are examples of **explicit** (or **declarative**) memories because they can be consciously recalled and described.

Procedural memory is a memory for skills and how to perform them. These memories can be demonstrated but may be rather difficult to put into words or be consciously described. For this reason, procedural memory is often considered a type of **implicit** (or **non-declarative**) memory because you may not need to consciously recall it in order to perform the behavior. In fact, you may not even be consciously aware that the memory exists. For instance, you can probably effortlessly tie your shoes, but if you were asked to consciously describe each step of tying your shoes, you might find it difficult. You may even need to perform the behavior and then narrate what you see your hands doing. This divide between our memory of how to do things and how to consciously describe how we do those things can provide insight into the complexity of teaching physical tasks. These different types of memory explain why someone may be able to perfectly execute a complex maneuver, but find themselves at a complete loss for words when it comes to describing exactly what they are doing.

Schacter's Seven Sins of Memory

Despite the shared terminology with computers, our memory doesn't work like a hard drive, neatly and accurately storing information to be called up later. Our memory is subject to error, either at the level of encoding, storage, or retrieval, resulting in several different types of failures, which Harvard professor **Daniel Schacter** refers to as the **"Seven Sins of Memory"**: Transience, Absentmindedness, Blocking, Misattribution, Suggestibility, Bias, and Persistence.

Transience is a failure of retrieval that results from the passage of time. The German researcher **Hermann Ebbinghaus** worked to quantify how much memory faded (and how quickly it faded) by repeatedly testing himself with lists of nonsense syllables made by placing a vowel between two consonants (creating "words" like DEK, PUV, DUT, etc.). Based on his data, he described a "*forgetting curve*" which showed that a great deal of information is lost rather quickly, and then the rate of information loss slows and the curve gradually flattens.

The inevitably transient nature of our memory highlights the importance of regular review for memories we wish to maintain. By repeatedly reviewing information, we can gradually raise the curve and increase our retention. In the Improve Your Memory section at the end of this chapter we'll go into more detail on how to maximize the effectiveness of your review to reduce transience.

Absentmindedness is a type of forgetting that occurs due to a lapse in attention. If you've ever forgotten an umbrella in a restaurant or a bag in a taxi, you've experienced absentmindedness. It generally isn't the case that the memory has been completely forgotten (since it is often recalled just moments later) but rather that our attention is momentarily placed elsewhere and so we fail to bring the memory to mind when we need it. We can think of this as a type of retrieval error, because even though the memory has been encoded and stored accurately (as evidenced by our later recall) we fail to retrieve the memory at the appropriate time.

Knowing that our future self may fail to remember something at the appropriate time and then making plans to prevent this from occurring is referred to as **prospective memory**; memory for the future. This is planning a reminder for something that will force our attention to retrieve the memory at the appropriate time. For instance, if you're worried about forgetting to bring an important bag with you tomorrow morning, you might place the bag in front of the door tonight. This will ensure that you see the bag as you are leaving in the morning, directing your attention to retrieve the appropriate memory (bring this with me) at the appropriate time (and not 20 minutes later when you are half-way to your destination).

Blocking occurs when we have a memory but are temporarily unable to successfully retrieve it. This may cause a "***tip-of-the-tongue*** *experience*"; the frustrating condition in which we know that the memory is there even though we can't bring it to mind. We know that we have encoded and stored the memory, so the error is at the level of retrieval. This tip-of-the-tongue experience can be triggered when we attempt to retrieve memories that are infrequently accessed, such as when trying to recall the word for a person who makes maps, or when trying to remember the name of a former classmate.

Misattribution occurs when we incorrectly identify where a memory came from. We have the memory, but we think it came from somewhere else. If you start telling a juicy story to a friend and are interrupted by "I'm the one who told you that yesterday", misattribution is to blame. Misattribution reveals that our brains aren't particularly good at ***source memory***, or memory for where information came from. So while we may correctly encode an interesting fact, we may have trouble recalling whether a friend told us, we read it on a blog, or saw it in a YouTube video. This memory error can be particularly troublesome in the courtroom, as eyewitnesses may incorrectly identify innocent bystanders as perpetrators (because they recognize their faces) or even falsely accuse others they recognize from completely different circumstances.

A famous (and somewhat ironic) example of this occurred when a woman accused Donald Thomson of rape. Thomson's alibi was sound, as he was at a television studio filming a live broadcast when the crime occurred. The woman had actually been watching the program prior to her attack, and she misattributed her memory of Thomson's face to that of her attacker. The irony is that in his television appearance, Thomson, a psychologist, was discussing eyewitness memory for faces.

Advertisers use our poor source memory to their advantage, as they blatantly sing the praises of their own products. While this type of blow-hard bravado may seem in poor taste, later we may recall hearing positive messages about a product, though we've forgotten that we heard those good things from the very company selling the product.

Misattribution can also occur in the form of ***false recognition***, when a novel stimulus is similar enough to a previously-seen stimulus that we think they are the same. So we may believe that we recognize someone or something that we haven't actually seen before. This false recognition has been proposed as one possible explanation for the phenomenon of *déjà vu*, as a new experience may trigger feelings of familiarity because it resembles a previous experience. In contrast, we may occasionally suffer from ***cryptomnesia***, when we believe that a thought is new, when actually it is a memory of an old thought. This can lead to inadvertent plagiarism; we think an idea came from our own creative processes, but in fact it is a memory of someone else's work. Authors and musicians may be heartbroken (and legally liable) upon the realization that a wonderful turn of phrase or catchy riff is not a sign of their genius and creativity, but rather, a sign of their source memory's fallibility.

Suggestibility is the idea that external information can infiltrate and modify our memories, even implanting memories that weren't there in the first place. In a number of studies, ***Elizabeth Loftus*** and colleagues have demonstrated that leading questions can change existing memories and false memories can be successfully created via suggestion. In one study, Loftus and John Palmer found that participants' estimates of vehicle speed in a video of a car accident were influenced by the use of "smashed" vs. "hit" in the question (speed estimates rose significantly when participants were asked about cars that "smashed into each other").

In another study, Loftus was able to successfully implant the false memory of being lost in a shopping mall as a child into the minds of several of her participants. These studies on suggestibility cast doubt on how much we can trust our own memories. We should remember that our memories are not recordings of events, but rather, ***reconstructions*** of events and we are always prone to the possibility of error each time we try to mentally put the pieces together.

Our memory is also subject to ***bias***. We tend to reconstruct our past so that it seems more like our present (known as ***consistency bias***) and we also tend to selectively recall memories that make us look better (known as ***egocentric bias***), such as when college students who were asked to recall their high school transcripts tended to successfully recall the high grades but forgot more of the low grades they had received. This may be a bias that's not so bad, as there might be practical implications for our self-esteem. Egocentric bias may help ensure we recall our previous successes and minimize our failures, helping us feel more capable and motivated.

The final "sin" of memory from Schacter's list is when intrusive memories are brought to mind repeatedly and without conscious control, known as **_persistence_**. Flashbacks of negative events and traumatic experiences can repeatedly disrupt the minds of victims, interfering with their lives. Persistence demonstrates the powerful and sometimes painful connection between emotion and memory. We may consider the role of persistence in syndromes such as Post-Traumatic Stress Disorder (**_PTSD_**) in which patients feel trapped reliving the same traumatic event over and over again.

Those with PTSD may represent the extreme of persistence but for all of us, emotional events tend to be remembered better than non-emotional events. This can be seen in **_flash-bulb memories_**; detailed memories of emotionally-charged events. I can recall exactly where I was on the morning of September 11, 2001, and that's an example of a flash-bulb memory. I can remember more details of that morning than some other non-emotionally-charged morning of say October 7, 2007. This isn't to say that my memories of September 11th aren't still subject to all of the other potential errors and biases above, but rather that the emotional intensity of that particular morning partially explains why it is more memorable and why memories of that particular morning may be brought to mind more often.

Our physical and emotional state plays a role not just in encoding memories, but also in their retrieval, as our current state prepares us to recall events from similar physical and emotional states. This is known as **_state-dependent memory_**. For example, when we're brimming with enthusiasm and motivation, we're more likely to recall memories filled with optimism and excitement, but when we're feeling down it's easier to recall past experiences of sadness and disappointment. This has important implications for the treatment of disorders like depression because it may contribute to a downward spiral as depressed patients are more likely to recall negative memories and experiences, further reducing their mood.

The Biology of Memory

One major breakthrough in understanding brain structures and memory came from the case of H.M., a patient who had the hippocampus surgically removed from both sides of his brain to reduce epileptic seizures. Following his surgery, which was successful in reducing seizures, H.M. was unable to form new memories, a condition known as ***anterograde amnesia***. While hippocampectomy is rare, other patients with hippocampal damage from injury or infection have provided similar case studies. These cases also provide evidence that long-term memory is a separate store of memory in the 3-box model, since these patients have intact sensory and short-term memory. They can repeat lists of words, copy diagrams, and answer questions, but they cannot move this information to long-term memory. Just moments later they won't remember the words in the list, the fact that they had been drawing, or even what question they are in the middle of answering.

There is some evidence, however, that they are able to retain some long-term memory in the form of ***procedural memories***. H.M. was able to improve his ability in certain types of physical tasks (such as drawing while looking in a mirror) even though he couldn't consciously remember practicing the tasks. It appears that the cerebellum, basal ganglia, and striatum are crucial structures in the formation and storage of these types of procedural memories, which is why H.M. was still able to learn them despite lacking functioning hippocampi.

The case of Clive Wearing, a British musicologist who received damage from a brain infection, is even more severe, because in addition to anterograde amnesia he suffers extensive ***retrograde amnesia***, or loss of existing memories. He has almost no prior declarative memories, and, being unable to form new memories, this leaves him with only the present moment. He has functioning sensory memory and short-term memory, but no ability to create new long-term memories and very little ability to retrieve old long-term memories. This means that he is mentally living in a brief window of time, lasting only a matter of seconds. He does have procedural memories intact, as he can still speak and use language correctly, walk and move normally, and even play the piano. As with the cases above, this suggests that procedural memories must be stored and organized differently than other types of long-term memory.

Neural Mechanisms of Memory

Synaptic activity between two neurons can lead to a strengthened connection between those two neurons, known as **Long-Term Potentiation (LTP)**. This is often summarized with the expression "neurons that fire together wire together". Even though these neurons don't actually "wire together" in terms of physically touching, the strength of their connection is increased via chemical interactions when they repeatedly fire synchronously. While the exact mechanisms of this process are not yet fully understood, there are several factors that are believed to be important. One possible signaling pathway is **NMDA,** for **N-methyl-D-aspartate,** a receptor for the neurotransmitter glutamate.

Repeated firing of a synapse causes the postsynaptic neuron to increase its number of glutamate receptors and this changes the postsynaptic neuron's sensitivity to future stimulation. Mice who have had an NMDA antagonist injected into their hippocampus have shown impaired spatial learning in a maze task (Morris, 1986). Ketamine, an anesthetic frequently used as a recreational drug, is an NMDA antagonist, explaining why one of its many effects is memory loss.

Understanding the neural aspects of memory formation also opens the possibility for the development of drugs to improve our memories. Mice given boosts to their NMDA levels show improved performance in learning tasks, so we may wonder whether human memory drugs will be hitting pharmacy shelves in the not-too-distant future. Until that day arrives, however, we'll need to rely on other methods of improving our memory, and fortunately humans actually have thousands of years of experience in this department.

How to Improve Your Memory

My hope is that this section of the book is the most valuable and will help you to recall and apply the material from all of the other chapters. I think that it's best to have background understanding of the preceding material in this chapter first, so if you haven't already read the first half of this chapter, I highly recommend you do so before reading this section, as much of the terminology used here is explained there. Now let's look at how we can leverage our knowledge of memory to improve our ability to retain information. Along the way we'll learn a few more terms for some memory concepts, but with a focus on how they can be applied to mastering our own memory.

I want to keep this section practical and applicable, so I'm going to step back from explaining the details of the research supporting these principles. That said, if you are interested in more of the technicalities of this type of memory research, I encourage you to check the references section, where I've listed supporting studies for these concepts.

The Importance of Organization

One of the first steps to improving memory is to organize the information that we want to recall. If I need to buy 15 items from the grocery store, rather trying to remember all items in a haphazard manner, organizing them by category would immediately improve my chances of recalling them correctly. Chunking these items into groups like vegetables, prepackaged foods, beverages, etc. provides a hierarchical structure that has been demonstrated to improve recall. Waiters and waitresses often use the same technique, organizing items by category, rather than blindly sticking to the mismatched sequence of items as customers placed their orders.

This may seem fairly obvious when it comes to grocery lists and entrees, but this organizational encoding can and should be applied to just about anything you want to remember. If you're looking to learn a bunch of SAT words you might start by organizing them into categories of nouns, verbs, and adjectives or maybe you'd prefer to break them into groups based on positive and negative connotations. There are any number of groupings that might make sense, you just want to avoid a chaotic jumble of terms.

While I've tried to organize terms in this book by related concepts, you might find that you remember them better by focusing on key individuals and the terms necessary for talking about their work. The type of organization you prefer is personal, but the key point is that you should have a structure in place. Later, once you have a good grasp of most of the information, you can shuffle your flashcards or pick out random terms to mix things up but this should be during review, not initial learning.

Breaking it Down with Ebbinghaus

In the section on transience, we learned about the forgetting curve that Hermann Ebbinghaus created, but what wasn't mentioned is that Ebbinghaus also found recall tended to be better for certain items based on their location in his lists. He found that he was better able to recall the items at the beginning and the end of a list, known as the ***serial position effect***. Improved recall for the initial items on a list is known as ***primacy***, while the improvement for the final items of the list (which are most recent) is referred to as ***recency***.

Imagine that you had a list of 20 items you wanted to recall. Serial position effects mean that you might recall the first few and last few terms better, but what about the 15 or so in the middle? Simply by breaking this list into 2 groups of 10 items, you'd be doubling your primacy and recency effects. And if you were to break those two lists down into smaller lists of just 5 items, you'd probably find your recall substantially improved without spending more time reviewing.

This is why it's important to take frequent breaks and to study material in small sections. Not only is it easier to stay focused and maintain your attention, but you also get the benefit of having more first items and more last items. Keep this in mind when you make your overly-ambitious study plans which include marathon cramming sessions. Rather than planning to slog your way through an entire book at once, plan to read just one section, then break, then return for the next section, etc. Provided that you keep returning (and those breaks don't turn into 4 hours of video games) you'll probably find that you're able to recall more of the material even after just one reading.

Testing Yourself

Students around the world may groan when they hear this, but testing does actually have benefits for memory, provided that you get a chance to see the answers and get feedback on your responses. This type of testing + feedback has been shown to improve recall more than simply having another review session and the resulting memory boost is known as the ***testing effect***. We should take advantage of this by making all our review a type of test. This is why flashcards can be so much more effective than simply re-reading definitions. By forcing yourself to come up with an answer every time and then getting immediate feedback, you're able to get the testing effect many times over.

It's also a good idea to review often and in short sessions. This is known as *distributed review* and it has been shown to be more effective than long sessions or *massed practice*. Each time we review we raise that forgetting curve and slow the rate of its decline. There are a number of programs available which can schedule your review for you, known as *spaced-repetition software* or *SRS* (I personally use Anki and can recommend it). These programs calculate your next review based on your ranking of how well you remembered an item.

If you're sure that you've really learned everything, don't stop just yet. There's actually good reason to continue to review. Ebbinghaus found that transience decreased when he continued to review material that he already knew. This is known as *overlearning* and it should actually be a part of your study plans. Hopefully this will help you to pass your exams, but more importantly, help you to recall the material long after the exams have passed.

Go Deep

Information which is more deeply processed tends to be remembered better, known as *levels of processing theory*. This deeper processing refers to considering the information, and reflecting or analyzing how it may fit in with other memories and experiences. This is something that I've tried to naturally incorporate throughout this text.

Rather than simply listing terms and definitions, I've tried to connect ideas and explain why particular concepts are so important. This technique is strengthened when information can be made more personal. This is known as the *self-referential effect*. Connecting something to your own personal sense of self strengthens your ability to recall it. For instance, if you were trying to remember a random list of words and one was *chihuahua*, and you have many fond memories with your pet chihuahua, chances are good that you would remember this word better than the others on the list. Thinking of ways you've personally experienced classical conditioning, vicarious reinforcement, or memory failures will strengthen your ability to recall and apply these concepts.

Create Retrieval Cues

Retrieval cues are related memories that can help us to retrieve a particular memory. You probably use these quite often when you are having trouble recalling something. Imagine that someone has asked you the name of an actor who starred in a particular movie. You know the actor, but you're experiencing **blocking** and can't come up with his name. You may begin searching your memory for retrieval cues such as other movies that he has starred in. These other movie titles, though they don't feature the actor's name, can serve as retrieval cues because they may be mentally connected to the actor's name. Our related memories tend to form networks of connections to one another, so recalling one can help to activate another.

Similarly, I might ask you to read the following list:

hospital, nurse, sick, bed, stethoscope, physician, medicine, exam, gown

Now if tomorrow I were to ask you to recall as many words from the list as possible, there's a high likelihood that you would recall the word "doctor", even though it wasn't on the list. Because I activated many words related to "doctor", it may feel as if doctor itself was activated. This *spreading activation* of memory can be used to our advantage by activating as many related memories as possible for something that we want to recall. While in the case above recalling "doctor" would be an error, if we really wanted to recall the word doctor tomorrow then reading this list would be an excellent way to help make that happen.

Sleep and Memory Consolidation

As we'll see in chapter 4, there is a strong relationship between sleep and memory. Sleep seems to play a key role in consolidating our memories while sleep deprivation has clearly been shown to wreak havoc on our ability to form new memories. We'll look at some of the evidence in chapter 4, but for now, suffice to say that getting enough sleep is fundamental to maximizing your memory powers. Long, late nights of cramming might not be nearly as effective as shorter sessions followed by plenty of sleeping time.

The Method of Loci

This technique is perhaps the most important concept in this book and it has the potential to truly transform your ability to remember. The beauty of this mnemonic technique is that it is incredibly simple and requires only minimal preparation to implement.

The method of loci (sometimes called the **Journey Method**, or the **Roman Room method**) has been used for thousands of years and consists of mentally traveling along a familiar route and placing mental images at different locations (*loci* in Latin) as you go. These mental images represent the information to be remembered, and by using a familiar route, the order of the information will naturally be preserved.

This technique can truly revolutionize your memory abilities. While entire books have been written on the subject of memory improvement, I believe that the method of loci is the most efficient and practical technique that can be taught, and it can be learned in minutes. Of course, practice is necessary to really unlock the potential power of this technique.

First, you need a journey that you know well, such as your home or apartment. Now, let's say that you wanted to remember the 12 animals of the Chinese zodiac, in order. They are:

Rat, Ox, Tiger, Rabbit, Dragon, Snake, Horse, Goat, Monkey, Rooster, Dog, Pig

In order to quickly memorize this list, you could use your home or apartment and come up with 12 locations (in order) to place each animal. Perhaps you start at your bed, imagining it covered with rats (certainly a memorable, if unpleasant, image), then you'd move to the next location, perhaps a table next to your bed. Imagine a giant ox carefully balanced on the table, trying not to fall off and wake you. Then perhaps you move to the closet where you part the clothes to find a tiger staring you in the face, ready to pounce. As you continue through the natural sequence of your home, you use your imagination to create vivid images.

When you've finished, you'll find that simply mentally traveling through your house will bring each animal to mind. It won't feel like you're "studying" the list at all, but you'll be able to bring it to mind nearly effortlessly. The order of the list will naturally be preserved because the order of rooms won't suddenly change. Now the only limit to how many items you can recall is how many locations your journey has (and how much time you want to spend creating images). This method has been used by world champion memorizers to recall tens of thousands of items.

If you want to remember something permanently you'll still need to review it, and this means you give it a dedicated journey that isn't used for anything else. So if I had 20 products I want to always have mentally ready for work, I might use 20 locations around my workplace for those items and those items only. Then I could effortlessly rattle off all 20 products in order without worrying about leaving any out.

For other information that you only need to remember for a short time, you can use a journey, then reuse that journey later for new information. This multi-purpose journey is like a mental USB drive that you might keep documents on for short periods, constantly swapping things in and out. Just mentally clearing out a journey (by imagining the locations empty) is generally enough to allow you to refill it with new images.

I personally use my childhood home frequently for information that I want to remember short-term but don't need long-term. I use this journey to do memory demonstrations in my classes, in which case I may only need to remember the information (such as a random list of words) for an hour or so. After the demonstration is over and I don't need to remember the info, I simply don't review it. Next time I do a demonstration, I can use the same journey locations again because the old associations have faded.

I believe that when used effectively, the method of loci can incorporate many mnemonic techniques in one and this is what gives it tremendous power. I'd like to briefly outline how all the factors we've learned already can apply to the Method of Loci and why it's the first mnemonic technique I'd recommend to anyone looking to improve memory.

Creating a journey immediately imposes a structure (***organizational encoding***) and it relies on mental images (known as ***visual imagery encoding***). The Method of Loci forces you to consider the information and connect it to something that you already know (in this case, a familiar journey). This means that you are processing the information more deeply, and this in itself should help to make it more memorable (***levels of processing theory***). You can add to this effect by considering any emotional response for the image you have created. What other senses and emotions does it evoke (***state-dependent memory***)? Regardless of emotional impact, the images and relationships you create will be personal (***self-referential effect***). Even when we struggle to recall something in a journey, the location serves as a vivid starting point to help us (***retrieval cue***). In addition, this method allows us to review materially mentally by going through our journey so we can review often (***spaced repetition***) and each time we mentally reach a location and try to recall the image we are testing ourselves (***the testing effect***).

All of these factors have me convinced that the Method of Loci is the most versatile and effective mnemonic tool for improving memory. But you may not be convinced just yet.

What about things that aren't easily visualized?

This might appear to be the Achilles' Heel for this technique, but fortunately it is a weakness that can be overcome. When faced with items that are hard to visualize (like foreign words, numbers, or abstract ideas) we need to apply additional systems in order to place mental images along our journey. This isn't as hard as it might seem, though creating images will require some creativity.

Sound-alikes - This is sometimes referred to as the ***Link Method*** or the ***Keyword method*** and it's useful for things that don't have mental images associated with them, such as the sounds of a foreign word. In this case, a mental image is created based on similar sounds that will help link the original word with its definition. For example, if you were learning that the Spanish word for beer is *cerveza*, you might realize that *cerveza* sounds a bit like "survey sir" (not exactly, but close enough to cue your memory). You might imagine someone sitting in a bar, and rather than bringing a nice cold beer, the waiter brings a survey to complete, saying "survey, sir". This mental image might be just enough to remind you that the word for beer is *cerveza*.

While this technique isn't going to work for every new word you encounter, it can help if you've got a lot of terms to learn. You may even find that just trying to create the sound-alikes will force you to engage with the words and consider self-referential images for remembering them, which certainly won't hurt your chances of correct recall. While this method is often touted as a stand-alone technique, I find it combines quite well with the method of loci because placing the images you create along a journey will help to ensure that you review them and will also provide additional structure to help you retrieve them.

Number Systems

One way to visualize numbers is to use a shape system that creates a visual image for each digit. 0 could be an egg, 1 a baseball bat, 2 a swan, 3 a pair of breasts(!), 4 a sailboat, 5 a hook, 6 a golf club, 7 an axe, 8 a snowman, and 9 a balloon on a string. Now, rather than trying to remember whether a digit was a 4 or a 5, you'll have very different mental images that are less likely to be confused. When confronted with the task of remembering a number you can place a mental image of each digit along a mental journey, just as you did for the animals in the zodiac. Then when you recall the images, just translate back into numbers.

If there were a number that I wanted to permanently commit to memory, I would give it its own journey which is not used for any other information. I've memorized my passport number by using a journey through an airport security check, placing images in the little plastic bin, the x-ray machine, the metal detector, the "wand area", the end of the conveyor belt, etc. For memorizing a friend's telephone number, you might use their apartment as the journey for the images.

If you're more ambitious, you can try tackling a more complex number system, creating a mental image for every two-digit number. So you'll have a visual image you can bring to mind for all numbers from 00 to 99. This cuts the number of images that you need in half (though it does take a little more time to create and practice with) and adds the advantage of *chunking*, allowing you to remember numbers in groups rather than single digits. This is a system that I use to memorize numbers and I have a "character" that I bring to mind for each pair of digits. Rather than randomly selecting a person for each number, I populated my list by using a system of name initials shown below.

0=O   1=A   2=B   3=C   4=D   5=E   6=S   7=G   8=H   9=N

This is known as the Dominic System, after Dominic O'Brien, world memory champion and author of several excellent books on memory training. I first learned this system many years ago from one of O'Brien's books on mnemonic systems and methods for memorizing numbers, cards, dates, and more.

So in my list, each two-digit number becomes a set of initials, which then becomes a visual image of a person. If I wanted to recall 341630, the number 34 (CD) becomes Cameron Diaz. 16 (AS) becomes Arnold Schwarzenegger, while 30 (CO) calls up an image of Conan O'Brien. Now when faced with the task of memorizing a long string of digits, I just need to convert each pair to a person and place it along my mental journey. When faced with an odd number of digits, I combine this pair-system with the shape system above, which is only used for the final (single) digit.

If you want to really get extreme, you can also add an action for each character, and then an object as well, so that now each single mental image can store 6 digits (first two digits – person, next two digits – action of second person, next two digits – associated object of third person). So 341630 would become a single image of Cameron Diaz (*person*), flexing her muscles (*action* for Arnold), while holding an Eisenhower coffee mug (*object* for Conan).

This advanced person-action-object technique is mostly for the hardcore mnemonists looking to compete, but it can be used by anyone who has reason or inclination to memorize long strings of digits on a regular basis. The people, actions, and objects are highly personal, and as a result, the above may not make much sense to anyone but me so the biggest time commitment comes in creating your own personalized people, actions, and objects.

Even if you aren't looking to get this deep into the bizarre world of mnemonic techniques, I encourage you to learn the basics of the Method of Loci and apply it whenever you need to memorize something. You might be surprised at just how well your memory works.

A Memorable Example

Let's end with a more practical example and say that you wanted to memorize Schacter's Seven Sins of Memory from earlier in this chapter. All you would need to do is create a mental image for each sin, then place each image along a 7-location journey. Here's some ideas for visual images for each: **Transience** (a transient hobo), **Absentmindedness** (Fred McMurray as the absent-minded professor – or Robin Williams in the remake *Flubber*), **Blocking** (a large block of wood), **Misattribution** (a blurry-faced mugshot), **Suggestibility** (a smashed-up car from Loftus and Palmer's study), **Bias** (a scale of justice heavily tipped to one side), and **Persistence** (a melting watch from Salvador Dali's *The Persistence of Memory*). It takes a bit of work and imagination to create these images, but once you have done it the time you'll save on mindless studying will be more than worth it.

Now if you placed these images along a short journey, you could review these seven sins any time you wanted, without needing to carry around flashcards or a bulky textbook. With enough practice, eventually you'd easily recall them without even needing to think of the journey at all.

Chapter Summary – Memory

- The ***3-Box Information Processing Model*** divides memory storage into ***sensory memory***, ***short-term memory***, and ***long-term memory***.

- Daniel Schacter has described memory failures as the 7 "sins" of memory: ***Transience***, ***Absentmindedness***, ***Blocking***, ***Misattribution***, ***Suggestibility***, ***Bias***, and ***Persistence***.

- Memories can be categorized as ***explicit*** or ***implicit***, depending on our level of conscious awareness. Within these categories, memories can also be labeled as ***episodic***, ***semantic***, or ***procedural***.

- Emotion and memory are closely linked, and this link can be seen in ***persistence***, ***flash-bulb memory*** and ***state-dependent memory***.

- Evidence from case studies of patients like H.M. and Clive Wearing highlights the role of the ***hippocampus*** in memory formation. At the neural level, ***long-term potentiation*** refers to strengthening of synaptic connections between neurons after they repeatedly fire together.

- Memory can be improved through the use of mnemonic strategies such as the ***method of loci***, ***visual imagery encoding***, ***chunking***, and ***spaced-repetition***.

Notes

Chapter 3
Language and Cognition

How Do We Acquire Language?

In 1957, B. F. Skinner published *Verbal Behavior*, an explanation of language acquisition according to behaviorist principles of reinforcement and punishment. Skinner believed that language acquisition could be understood in the same way that lever pressing and disc pecking was understood. Children were reinforced for proper language use, and ignored or punished for improper use, and the buildup of all these consequences eventually led to their full development of linguistic capabilities.

Noam Chomsky, a young linguist at MIT, was not convinced by Skinner's explanations and in 1959 wrote a scathing review which argued that Skinner's claims about language acquisition were unsupported speculations. While Chomsky's review was not without critics of its own, this fiery attack of an icon of behaviorism has been suggested to have played a role in the cognitive revolution that followed. Beginning in the 1960s psychologists shifted their focus away from observable behaviors and onto internal mental processes.

In considering internal processes in language acquisition, Chomsky argued that humans must have a "***Language Acquisition Device***" (***LAD***). This isn't necessarily a brain structure or particular gene sequence, but rather a term for some device, system, or network in the human brain that allows language ability to emerge as long as there is sufficient input. Chomsky claimed that humans have this LAD and other animals don't, which explains why nearly all human children develop linguistic abilities almost effortlessly, while even years of intensive training is not able to effectively condition complex language use in animals.

The Building Blocks of Language

In order to better understood critiques of the behaviorist approach, we need to know a little bit more about ***linguistics***, the study of language.

All spoken languages are made up of individual sounds, though the sounds used in each language may vary. Some sounds (like the rolled Rs in Spanish or clicking sounds in Xhosa) may be somewhat unique, while other sounds may be shared among many languages. These small units of sounds that are used in a language are called ***phonemes***. Examples of phonemes in English would be sounds like the f sound in **f**at or the c sound in **c**at. English uses about 40 phonemes in total, while other languages may have twice this amount, or may manage to get by with just over a dozen.

While phonemes like **f** and **c** don't mean anything on their own, language also contains small units that are meaningful. These meaningful units are referred to as ***morphemes***. (You can remember that morpheme starts with **m**, and **m**orphemes have **m**eaning). Morphemes can be as small as one letter like **a**, or they can be short words that cannot be further broken down into smaller meaningful parts, like **bat**. Morphemes also include suffixes and prefixes that affect meaning, like **pre**-, **post**-, -**ism**, or even just an -**s** at the end of a word to make it plural. So we might have one word composed of multiple morphemes, like **bats** (two morphemes: bat and -s), or **batman** (two morphemes: bat and man). Just as a limited number of phonemes can create thousands of morphemes, these morphemes can be combined to create many more thousands of different words (as evidenced by the 616,500+ word-forms you can find in the Oxford-English Dictionary).

When combining multiple sounds from phonemes and morphemes to create words there are certain rules. Each language has different rules for how its phonemes and morphemes can be combined and how these combinations are spoken. These rules are known as ***phonological rules***. Violation of these rules in a particular language results in an ***accent***, which may be characteristic of a particular region. For example, a regional Boston accent, often demonstrated with the sentence "Park the car in Harvard Yard", is known for dropping **r** sounds when they follow vowels, resulting in something like "Pahk the cah in Hahvahd Yahd". In this case, a Bostonian is combining phonemes in a manner that doesn't follow the phonological rules of standard English.

Accents that arise when learning a new language may occur because people are carrying over phonological rules from their native language, or because they have difficulty recognizing or producing the combinations of phonemes of the new language. For example, native Mandarin speakers may have trouble pronouncing English words that end in "L", because Mandarin doesn't use this phoneme in this way (L sounds are always followed by a vowel – like in *la, le, li, lu*). If you've seen the show *An Idiot Abroad*, now you can better understand the difficulty that Karl Pilkington had with Chinese speakers always calling him "Karl**a**".

Now that we have phonemes and morphemes and rules for combining them to make words, we need to have a set of rules for how to combine these words into meaningful phrases and sentences. These are ***syntactical rules***. These aren't the nit-picking grammatical rules from your English class, but the more general rules for the order of words and using tenses to communicate meaning.

Universal Grammar

Chomsky proposed a theory of "***universal grammar***" which suggests that the overall brain mechanisms for understanding and processing human language are the same for any language and therefore must be an innate human characteristic. Since children everywhere seem to automatically learn the language around them, regardless of what that language is, it seems that understanding of the general rules of how language works will naturally arise in any child exposed to language. In this respect, language seems different from the acquisition of other concepts like mathematical understanding. For example, intuitive understanding of concepts of grammar will emerge naturally starting around age 2 in just about everyone given language exposure. We don't see similarly rapid and near-universal understanding in other areas, suggesting a unique biological predisposition for concepts of grammar.

Many people misunderstand the concept of universal grammar. It's not saying that languages all share the same grammatical rules. It's saying that human languages all follow similar types of rules in their overall structure because all human languages are created and used by human brains. All those brains innately conceive of language working in the same way.

So while languages may differ in where they place subjects and objects, whether they conjugate verbs or not, or how they structure the future tense, these are just minor details compared to the overall structure of how language works. The concept of universal grammar points out that although languages differ in the details, they all have ways of indicating the concepts of nouns, verbs, and adjectives because these are the structures necessary for human brains to communicate linguistically. Unlike other animals, we seem to be born prepared for language, and this innate predisposition allows us to learn language rapidly.

Language Development

The rate of vocabulary growth in children is truly phenomenal. Between the ages of 1 and 5, children will acquire a vocabulary of thousands of words, at an average rate of around 10 words per day; far too quickly for reinforcement to effectively condition in such a short time. Part of this explosion of vocabulary growth comes from **fast-mapping**; the ability to connect a word with a meaning after only a single exposure. So when Mom is in the grocery store and says "this is an *apple*", the child is able connect these new sounds "*apple*" with this new object. Without any further reinforcement, the child may see an apple a week later, and correctly name it.

Children also develop an understanding of syntax quite rapidly. Children begin babbling at around 4 months old, and by the age of about 1 year children generally begin speaking single words, usually nouns. This is actually quite impressive because it demonstrates their understanding of the concept of nouns from all the other words and sounds they have heard.

Around age 2, children begin stringing words together into short sentences of just 2 words, known as **telegraphic speech**. These mini-sentences leave out function words like *the, an, a*, etc. and only include the most important words for communicating (like a telegraph message). This indicates that children are already able to identify which words really matter and which words are just grammatical fluff. These two word sentences show further evidence of grammatical understanding because they tend to follow the syntax of the child's native language.

Young English speakers, for instance, will say things like "want cookie" rather than "cookie want", following the general rule of placing an object after a verb in English. They will also say things like "big dog", placing the adjective before the noun, while their Spanish-speaking counterparts are saying "*perro grande*", reversing the order to follow the syntax of Spanish. Even these tiny fragments reveal that children are already picking up the rules of the language around them.

Around age 4 or 5, children begin making grammatical errors. These errors actually provide evidence that children are learning the rules of language rather than simply imitating others. At this age, children make errors such as saying "She *hitted* him" or "He *runned* to school". These errors reveal two important things. The first is that children have acquired an understanding of how the language works without necessarily having explicit grammar instruction. This **overgeneralization** of a rule reveals that the children actually understand the "-ed makes the past tense" rule, even though they are misapplying it.

Secondly, overgeneralization (also sometimes referred to as *overregularization*) supports the idea that language isn't learned by conditioning because these new errors have not been reinforced in the past (or even heard, since Mom and Dad never say things like "goed" or "bringed").

Another well-known demonstration that children are discovering the rules of language is known as **The Wug Test**, created by Jean Berko Gleason. In this test, children are introduced to a novel word by being shown a picture or toy called a "wug". Then when another wug is presented, the children complete the sentence "Here are two ___". The fact that young children can correctly complete the sentence with "wugs" means that they understand the concept of pluralization of nouns, even though they haven't been explicitly taught this rule and they've never heard anyone else say "wugs". Overgeneralization and the Wug Test demonstrate that a child is actively working out the rules of language, not simply parroting back phrases. This process of working out the rules seems to occur naturally with exposure to language.

There is, however, a clock ticking on this natural process of figuring out the grammatical rules of a language. In order for this to occur, it seems that a child must have exposure to a language before some time around age 7. Without exposure before this time, a *critical period* has passed and the development of full fluency in language is no longer possible.

This can be seen in the tragic cases of children deprived of language exposure for many years. Genie was a girl who was kept in isolation by her father, who didn't speak to her at all, from when she was 20 months old until she was rescued at the age of 13. Despite intensive efforts to teach Genie language, she was never able to develop a high level of competency. A similar case involved a girl named Isabelle who was kept in silent isolation until she was 6 years old. Following her rescue, however, Isabelle was able to make a full recovery and in fact within 1 year of instruction her language abilities were within a normal range.

It's important to remember that this critical period refers to ability for language and grammar in someone's first language, not a second (or third or fourth) language. It's not stating that if you haven't learned a particular language before age 7 that you can't learn it. But you have to have learned your **first** language by this point in order for your brain to develop the ability to process the rules of any language.

It seems that if children have had sufficient exposure to any language, this equips their mind to understand the concepts of grammatical rules, which in turn allows them to learn other languages in the future, even if the specific grammatical rules of the next language are completely different. While it is true that younger age in starting a second language is associated with the attainment of higher levels of fluency, it is still possible for people to achieve high levels of proficiency and fluency in another language, even if they begin learning at a later age.

There are some people, however, for whom naturally understanding the rules of grammar just doesn't seem to happen. These are people with *genetic dysphasia*, a rare condition in which a person is unable to learn the rules of grammar in his or her native tongue. Despite being able to learn complex ideas and use advanced vocabulary, these people are seemingly unable to work out the rules of grammar and repeatedly make errors. This suggests that language is a specialized module, unrelated to other types of learning and cognitive skills. In this way, the fact that people with genetic dysphasia can't seem to learn grammar provides further evidence that, for most people, acquiring language is an innate and near-automatic process.

The Importance of the Social Environment

The evidence for critical periods and the importance of exposure to language at a young age both suggest that the social environment is a crucial component of the language acquisition process. With this in mind, we shouldn't adopt a strictly nativist approach, but should instead adopt an *interactionist approach* to consider how our genetic predisposition for language interacts with our environment to allow for the complete development of linguistic fluency.

One of the most startling cases of how our social environment allows language to develop comes from Nicaragua. Following a revolution in 1980, the government in Nicaragua created schools for the deaf in the capital city of Managua. For the first time, deaf children from remote areas all over the country were brought together and given instruction in sign language.

Previously, many deaf children had been deprived of a full language environment in their hometowns and had only learned to communicate with family and friends via simple gestures. Without a formal sign language in place and deprived of a social environment which would allow them to communicate with others, these children never developed full linguistic fluency and concepts of syntax. With the new school, however, the hope was that deaf children could be taught an existing sign language, learn vocational skills, and become more independent members of society. Hopes for these lofty goals were questioned, however, as initial attempts to teach a formal sign language failed.

What happened instead was even more exciting. By placing all these young children together in the same environment, with a strong desire to communicate with one another, a new language began to emerge. While these gestures were initially dismissed as mere miming and mimicry, this turned out to be more than just playground slang. It was a fully functional language that naturally emerged, complete with all the syntactical rules, tenses, and other grammatical features you would find in any other language. This case shows us that the human mind has a natural drive to communicate and create structured language. So while you may think that grammatical rules were created to punish you in English class, the truth is that grammar is a naturally-emerging phenomenon that allows us to communicate more fully with others.

Does Language Influence How You Think?

One puzzling question that arises when thinking about language is how language and thought are related. When we see deaf adults from Nicaragua who were too late for the development of full language abilities, we may wonder just what their thoughts are like. Our own thoughts are so intertwined with our language that it may seem impossible to separate the two. For most of us, it often seems that all the thoughts we have occur in the form of words and we may wonder how those words influence our ways of thinking about the world.

The notion that our native language influences how we perceive the world is known as the ***linguistic relativity hypothesis***. It is also referred to as the ***Whorf-Sapir hypothesis***, based on the work of Benjamin Whorf and his mentor Edward Sapir. Whorf proposed that due to the grammatical structures of their language, speakers of the Hopi language conceptualized time differently than English speakers.

Whorf's views (published in the late 1930s and early 1940s) were heavily criticized throughout the 1960s (likely due to the dominance of the view of universal grammar) but have recently been re-examined and some psychologists are reconsidering the possible role of language on how we think about the world. While few would suggest that our language determines our thought, researchers have studied how the language we speak may influence our perception and memory for colors, objects, and time, though results have been mixed.

We also see the question of how language and thought are related in the form of popular articles listing "untranslatable" foreign words, often suggesting that speakers of these languages conceptualize the world in ways that other speakers don't. We may wonder, however, if this is actually the case, since while these terms cannot be reduced down to single words in other languages, they can most certainly be described (or else the article couldn't be written). This would suggest that even if we don't speak the language we can still have the same types of thought. Just because English doesn't have a single word for *schadenfreude* doesn't mean that I can't conceptualize (or even experience) taking joy in the suffering of others.

One of the problems with analyzing how language influences thought is that language is such an integral part of culture. We may readily admit that culture influences how we think, but it can be difficult or impossible to determine exactly how language fits in to this interaction. One way of attempting to separate language from culture is to look at people who live in similar cultures but speak different languages. For instance, I could look to a country like Switzerland and find native speakers of French, German, Italian, and Romansh who, apart from language, arguably have rather similar cultural environments.

In addition to considering how language influences thought between individuals, we can consider how language may influence thought *within* individuals. In bilingual individuals who speak both languages fluently, perhaps their thinking varies when using one language or another. Several studies have investigated this, with some surprising results. Research by Michael Ross, Elaine Xun, and Anne Wilson in 2002 found that bilingual Chinese/English speakers described their personality traits quite differently depending on the language they used for the description. Similarly, Nairán Ramírez-Esparza and colleagues published a study in 2006 looking at bilingual Americans and Mexicans and found variation in their personality scores for extraversion, agreeableness, and conscientiousness depending on whether they were assessed in English or Spanish.

While the linguistic relativity hypothesis considers thought across languages, we may also wonder how language influences thought within a particular language. Does Orwellian "newspeak" really influence how people think about important issues? Does the fact that Beijing media refers to the city's pollution as 雾霾 *wu mai* (literally "fog-haze") rather than using the general term for pollution 污染 *wu ran* (literally "dirty contamination") influence how the city's residents perceive their environment? As we've already seen in memory experiments by Elizabeth Loftus, and as we'll see in framing studies by Amos Tversky and Daniel Kahneman in the next section, it does seem to be the case that particular wording has the potential to influence thought and decision-making, though the extent of this influence is still up for debate.

Concepts and Categories

Language provides us with ways of organizing thought, and one way that we see this organization is the creation of **concepts** and **categories**. These are mental groupings of objects or ideas which are similar. Rather than creating a completely new word for every possible shape of a chair, we can use the generic word "chair" both to represent a particular chair, and the concept of a chair in general. The question is, how do our brains go about this organizational process? When we walk into IKEA, how do we immediately recognize that a stimulus we've never seen before is in fact a chair?

If we try to come up with the rules our brains are using to decide on "chair-ness", we find that it's no simple task. Must it have 4 legs? Well, some chairs don't have legs at all but have solid bases instead and we recognize those just the same. A soft or hard surface? Again, both seem acceptable, so that doesn't help us to create a rule. Sharp or rounded corners? None of these rules seem to work in helping us recognize chairs, and yet, we can almost always recognize any chair immediately upon seeing it. So if we aren't following specific rules, how are we doing this?

What seems to be happening is that we have some guidelines rather than rules. These guidelines are the features that are common to chairs, and when we think of a chair, we generally think of these characteristics. We seem to think of an idea of a chair that has most of these features, but we also recognize that there are exceptions and variations. In considering a new object, these guidelines come to mind, but we don't use them as hard-and-fast rules for making a judgment.

To demonstrate this, take a moment and quickly doodle a picture of a bird.

Do so now, before looking ahead ;)

Now, if my magical powers of intuition are correct, you may have drawn something like this:

Chances are that you didn't draw a penguin, or an ostrich, or a peacock. While all of these are fine examples of birds, they probably aren't the first birds that came to mind. What probably came to mind is a "most-typical" version of a bird. This most-typical or best example is known as a **prototype**. A prototype has many or all of the characteristic features that we associate with a particular category.

So for birds, your prototype is probably small, feathered, winged, able to fly, and has twig-like legs and a small beak. If, when walking in a park, you encounter a new stimulus that might be a bird, you mentally compare it to your prototype to see how well it fits this category. A bird that is a close match to your prototype would probably be recognized more quickly than one that differs drastically. The same would be true for recognizing chairs. You have a mental prototype of a chair with all the "most chair-like" features, and you compare new possible chairs to this mental image.

In attempting to explain category recognition, **exemplar theory** considers that we aren't limited to thinking just about prototypes, and we may also mentally compare a stimulus to other examples in memory (though this may take us a little longer). For chairs, this may allow you to recognize a soft lumpy mass as a chair, because you have a memory of beanbag chairs as a less-common but still acceptable type of chair. Or if you were to encounter a large, flightless animal, you could still consider the possibility that it is a bird, even though several features don't match your prototypical bird.

How Do We Solve Problems?

Our minds do quite a lot of problem solving on a regular basis, but how do we go about solving problems? For some problems, it turns out, we don't actually have to do much solving. If I were to ask you to solve 3 + 4, chances are that you don't actually need to solve it. Instead, you simply need to remember the answer that you figured out long ago. But when you were younger and still learning addition, you may have had to actually work out the solution, perhaps by counting on your fingers.

So our memory of solutions that have worked in the past can help us to solve problems that appear again, but the downside to this approach is that it makes us vulnerable to applying a solution that has worked in the past that won't necessarily work in the present. This tendency to think only of what has worked in the past is known as our **mental set**. As Abraham Maslow wrote: "I suppose it is tempting, if the only tool you have is a hammer, to treat everything as if it were a nail" (Maslow, 1966, p.15). Perhaps, like me, you've wasted a great deal of time trying old solutions on new problems because you were unable to think of the problems from a new perspective.

There's also a tendency to view tools as only being useful in the ways that we usually use them. This is known as **functional fixedness**. Let's say that you want to hang a picture on your wall but when you check your toolbox you realize you lent your hammer to a friend. You might not immediately realize that you could probably drive in the nail using the side of the wrench sitting in front of you. You might not immediately realize this solution because of the tendency to think of wrenches as being used for wrenching things, not for hammering them.

I'm not suggesting that functional fixedness is always a bad thing. In fact, this tendency to concentrate on the normal functions of objects and tools is probably a good thing. Sure you could also use your cell phone to drive in that nail, but in the process you'd probably ruin its ability to perform the functions that it was specifically designed for. Nevertheless, we should be aware of this tendency and consider when novel uses for tools might be beneficial.

A related concept here is the difference between convergent and divergent thinking. In **convergent thinking**, we move towards one single solution to a problem. So if you're solving an algebra equation, often there is only one solution and each step should move you towards that single solution. In our hammer example, convergent thinking answers the question "how do I hammer in a nail?" by pointing towards one solution: a hammer.

Divergent thinking, on the other hand, is for situations with many possible solutions, and one solution may not be at all related to the other solutions. For example, if I asked you to imagine all the possible uses of a hammer, you may think of using it as a paperweight, and a moment later you may think of using it to get an object that's just out-of-reach, even though these solutions don't have much in common.

Obstacles to Problem Solving

As we begin considering solutions to problems, we should be aware of our tendency towards *overconfidence*. We tend to think that our views and judgments are correct, even when they aren't and we can be more confident than correct. For instance, when attempting to spell difficult words participants who felt 100% sure they were correct were actually only correct about 80% of the time.

Of course, even now that we know about overconfidence, we might feel that this error only applies to other people, not us. If you believe that you're never overconfident, then you are probably both wrong and overconfident. This tendency to think that errors and biases are just other people's problems relates to another type of bias. If you ask people to estimate how their own traits and abilities compare to others (e.g. attractiveness, IQ, driving ability, etc.) what you will find is that most people believe themselves to be above average. This is, of course, a statistical impossibility, but that doesn't always factor in to people's self-assessments. This tendency to feel above-average is known as *illusory superiority* or *The Wobegon Effect*, named after the fictional town of Lake Wobegon from Garrison Keillor's *A Prairie Home Companion;* a place "where all the women are strong, all the men are good-looking, and all the children are above average."

The Wobegon Effect may actually be a part of our "psychological immune system". Perhaps the tendency to exaggerate our estimates of our own positive traits helps to keep us motivated and upbeat, and when combined with a sense of overconfidence, makes it easier to make decisions and more likely we take action toward our goals.

Belief Bias

It's not surprising that our beliefs can cloud our judgment, but we may not realize just how easily our pre-existing beliefs can disrupt our ability to think logically. Research by Jonathan Evans, Julie Barston, and Paul Pollard found that previously existing beliefs influenced subjects' ability to determine whether statements were logically valid or invalid. It seems that we have difficulty separating our beliefs from our analysis of logic and we may not be aware of this influence.

Not only are we unaware of how our beliefs can influence our reasoning, our beliefs are resistant to change. This is known as ***belief perseverance***. Even when we are confronted with contradictory evidence, it generally does little to change our beliefs. Lee Ross, Mark Lepper, and Michael Hubbard (1975) gave participants false feedback on their performance (to create a belief about their abilities) then revealed that the feedback was unrelated to their actual performance (contradictory evidence). They then asked participants to assess their own performance and found ratings which still matched the false feedback previously received. Participants who had been told they performed well stuck to the belief that they were good at the task, even though they knew the feedback hadn't been accurate.

I'd like to offer a personal example that many students will relate to and illustrates several of the ideas above. Just as students tend to be overconfident in how quickly they can complete assignments, I was overconfident in how quickly I could write this book. Each chapter took me much longer than I had expected. Nevertheless, as I began a new chapter, I once again believed that I would be able to finish rapidly, ignoring the contradictory evidence and maintaining my belief.

This tendency to cling to our existing beliefs can be dangerous when making important decisions like determining the innocence or guilt of criminal defendants. While we may hope to uphold the notion that everyone is innocent until proven guilty, once a person has been viewed as a prime suspect it may be difficult for judges, jurors, or witnesses to overcome an initial belief of guilt.

If you're looking for a way to avoid this potential trap, research by Charles Lord and colleagues may be able to help. Their research suggests that considering opposite findings may have a stronger corrective effect than simply trying to be unbiased. When evaluating studies on the death penalty, some participants were told to "ask yourself at each step whether you would have made the same high or low evaluations had exactly the same study produced results on the other side of the issue." Other participants were simply told to be as unbiased as possible. The "consider the opposite" participants showed less bias in their critical evaluations of the studies and their attitudes toward the death penalty did not become as polarized.

Problem Solving Approaches

When it comes to solving problems, there are different approaches that we can take. One way to solve a problem is to use an ***algorithm***. An algorithm is a step-by-step procedure that guarantees you will reach a solution. Imagine that I'm getting ready to go out, but I can't find my apartment keys. I know they must be somewhere in my apartment, because I previously used them to get inside. An algorithm which would guarantee finding the keys would be to start in one corner of my apartment and systematically move through every square inch of the apartment until the keys were found.

Even though this approach would guarantee finding my keys, it's probably not the approach I would actually use. Instead of using an algorithm, I would probably use a ***heuristic***. A heuristic is a mental shortcut that doesn't guarantee a solution, but works most of the time. In searching for my keys, a heuristic I might use is to look where I last remember having them. Now they may not actually be where I last remember having them, but it's still a good place to start, rather than beginning in a corner of the room and slowly moving inch-by-inch through the apartment.

Heuristics and Decision-Making

It turns out that our minds love using heuristics. We're generally willing to accept the trade-off of occasionally being wrong in order to get the benefit of being fast. Amos Tversky and Daniel Kahneman spent decades uncovering the heuristics we use by creating ingenious demonstrations of how these heuristics can lead us astray. Here are just a few of the questions that Tversky and Kahneman have posed to participants, along with descriptions of the heuristics they reveal. These studies show us the consistent pattern of errors we make, which can be likened to the way that visual illusions consistently fool our perception. Dan Ariely refers to these as "decision illusions", and unlike visual illusions, it can be difficult for us to realize when we are being fooled.

The Availability Heuristic

In their first study of the availability heuristic, Tversky and Kahneman asked participants to estimate whether English had more words that started with the letter **k** or more words that had **k** as the third letter. What do you think?

If you're like most participants in their study, you might guess that there are more words that start with k than words that have k as the third letter, when in fact this is not the case. The reason you might have misjudged is that you were probably able to bring to mind more examples of words that start with k. We don't usually bring words to mind based on their third letter, so naturally it was harder to think of those examples. Thinking of words that start with k probably seemed much easier, and as a result you may have felt that these words are more common. The ***availability heuristic*** says that we tend to estimate the frequency of events based on how easily we can come up with examples, or how "available" they are to our mind.

This tendency to assume that things which are more easily recalled are more frequent can be seen when we attempt to estimate the likelihood of events like terrorist attacks or plane crashes. Examples of these unfortunate events tend to spring to mind rather easily, and this may cause us to assume that these events occur more frequently than they actually do.

On the other hand, events and dangers which actually are more frequent may not come to mind quite so readily. So parents may fear letting their children walk to school because of highly-memorable news stories of child abductions, even though the risks posed by choking, drowning, or car accidents are far greater. Often it seems that the things we fear might kill us are not the things that are actually likely to kill us. As comedian Norm Macdonald noted, you spend time thinking "gee, I hope a terrorist doesn't attack and kill me", when it's far more likely that your own heart is what will attack and kill you.

That Sounds Like A ….

In another study, Tversky and Kahneman asked participants to read randomly selected assessments from 100 interviews with 70 engineers and 30 lawyers. Participants were then asked to guess the likelihood that the person in question was an engineer or a lawyer. So I might randomly pull out an assessment and tell you that Adam was described as particularly outgoing, interested in politics, and displayed skill in argument. Then you would guess the odds that Adam was a lawyer or an engineer. What do you think? Here's another example from one of Tversky and Kahneman's descriptions:

"Dick is a 30 year old man. He is married with no children. A man of high ability and high motivation, he promises to be quite successful in his field. He is well-liked by his colleagues." (Tversky and Kahneman, 1973)

What do you think about Adam and Dick? What do you think the odds are that Dick is an engineer?

You probably immediately thought of Adam as a lawyer but found Dick a little harder to pin down. Most people in the study figured there was equal chance that Dick was an engineer or a lawyer, and so they estimated the odds of him being an engineer at around 50%. If you thought the same way, you relied on the **Representativeness Heuristic** – estimating likelihood by using information from prototypes and ignoring more useful information about base rates. In this case you tried to match these profiles to your prototypes of engineers and lawyers, and in doing so, you ignored information that was more relevant. If 70 interviewees were engineers and the assessments were randomly selected, there is a 70% chance any selected profile is an engineer regardless of personality traits. So if you were betting on accuracy in this task, the smart money would always be on engineer.

The Framing Effect

Tversky and Kahneman also investigated how the framing of questions can influence our decision-making by giving two groups of participants the same decision to make, but with a slight change in wording. Participants were asked to imagine the outbreak of a rare virus in a village of 600 people. They were then asked to adopt a program to combat this threat.

One group of participants was told that Program A would save 200 lives, while Program B had a 1/3 chance of saving everyone, and a 2/3 chance of saving no one.

The other group was told that with Program A, 400 people would die, while Program B had a 1/3 chance no one would die and a 2/3 chance everyone would die.

As you can see, choices are mathematically-identical for both groups and the difference is how the options are framed: lives saved vs. deaths. When the choices were framed as "saving", Program A was popular, but when those same numbers were framed as how many would die, the riskier Program B was widely adopted. Tversky and Kahneman proposed that when we consider benefits we like certainty, but when we consider losses we're more likely to take risks.

We see the use of framing in everyday life as well. Medications and interventions emphasize their 70% effectiveness rate, rather than frame it as a 30% failure rate. Customers find it more appealing when gas stations offer a "cash discount" rather than a "credit card fee" and government agencies may find more popular support for programs that aim to "help the needy" rather than "provide welfare".

How we define options can have an effect on the decisions that are made and which choices seem preferable. Eric Johnson and Daniel Goldstein analyzed data on organ donation in countries across Europe and found that the major factor in how many people were willing to participate in the organ donation program was whether the sign-up form was an automatic opt-in or opt-out. If the default option was joining, membership in the program was high, nearly 100% in many countries, but when not joining was the default, membership rates were low. We may not like the realization that we are so easily influenced by default options and the choices that form-designers make for us, but the evidence certainly points us toward that conclusion.

The Sunk-Cost Fallacy

The final decision-making error that we'll address may be familiar to you already and is known as the ***sunk-cost fallacy***. This is the tendency to make present decisions based on previous investments. These previous investments may no longer have any actual bearing on the decision being made, but we seem to have a hard time letting them go. So gamblers and stock speculators may make increasingly risky bets in attempts to make up for past losses even though those past losses don't have any effect on their odds of winning the present bets.

Perhaps this shouldn't always be considered a fallacy, as there are certainly times that our previous investments rightly influence our present decisions but we should consider how we frame past events and how they may become a part of our decision-making. Abandoning relationships or quitting jobs on a whim may be situations in which we can be glad that our previous investments constrain our decisions and allow us to keep a cool head.

Part of the explanation for the sunk-cost fallacy is that we seem to have a tendency to keep a sort of mental accounting of costs that we've occurred for specific circumstances. Tversky and Kahneman (1981) demonstrated how different frames of our past experiences can influence our decisions by asking participants to consider the scenario below.

"Imagine that you have decided to see a play where admission is $10 per ticket. As you enter the theater you discover that you have lost a $10 bill. Would you still pay $10 for a ticket for the play?"

When given this question, 88% of participants said yes they would purchase the ticket. Other participants saw this version of events:

"Imagine that you have decided to see a play and paid the admission price of $10 per ticket. As you enter the theater you discover that you have lost the ticket. The seat was not marked and the ticket cannot be recovered. Would you pay $10 for another ticket?"

In this second case, only 46% of participants were willing to purchase the ticket. In both cases, the loss of $10 is identical. The difference is that in the second case people feel that they have already invested $10 in the play, so they are unwilling to pay twice for the same show. Tversky and Kahneman suggested that rather than a purely rational single mental account of gains and losses, we tend to keep separate mental accounts. In the second case, the mental "theater-cost account" is already at -$10, so purchasing a new ticket would put the account at -$20, which is deemed too expensive for the show. In the first case, however, the lost $10 was not considered as part of the theater cost, and as a result did not come to bear on the decision.

Is There a Silver Lining?

If all this discussion of our biases and errors is upsetting, it shouldn't be. Gerd Gigerenzer has suggested that rather than thinking of these heuristics as biases, we should consider them as tools. We should take a moment to consider just how amazing our information-processing abilities are. Our capabilities are truly astonishing, and the very fact that our brains can contemplate their own shortcomings should be enough to inspire hope. The better we understand our failures and biases, the better able we will be to create systems that will help us to overcome them. And for all the failures that heuristics bring, we shouldn't ignore just how helpful they are.

There are even situations in which having little information can actually be more helpful in guiding us to the right answer. Daniel Goldstein and Gerd Gigerenzer asked American and German participants to estimate whether San Diego or San Antonio had a higher population. 62% of Americans were able to correctly identify San Diego as more populous. Interestingly, 100% of the German participants answered correctly. Were these Germans more knowledgeable about the population of American cities? Nope. These Germans reported that they had never heard of San Antonio, but were at least familiar with the name of San Diego. Without any information about the population of San Antonio, they relied on the assumption that the city they had heard of was probably a larger one, and as a result they were guided to the correct answer. This ***recognition heuristic*** shows how our minds are able to make decisions based on very little information. Rather than being crippled by indecision, our minds gladly take shortcuts whenever possible and some of these shortcuts turn out to be rather effective.

It also seems that we can create these shortcuts for our decision-making with extensive practice. This allows us to effectively automate decisions and conserve valuable mental energy. Our constant search for mental shortcuts combined with extensive experience can create expertise that allows people to make lightning-fast decisions while still maintaining high levels of accuracy. Chess masters can quickly size up the correct move with just a brief glance at a game board, baseball players can tell a good pitch from a bad one and decide to swing in an instant, and chicken-sexers can identify male or female chicks based on ambiguous genitals in less than a second, without even knowing exactly how they do it.

So while heuristics do cause us to make errors in judgment, we shouldn't ignore their usefulness. These shortcuts help make the world more manageable and allow us to make thousands of decisions each day, and for the most part, the decisions we make are good ones. Instead of being overwhelmed by the constant influx of irrelevant information, we somehow manage to move along, and even with these flaws, the history of human existence has been a story of increasing knowledge and unceasing improvement. So in our quest for greater cognitive efficiency we may occasionally stumble, but we shouldn't ignore the times when these shortcuts allow us to leap.

Chapter Summary – Language & Cognition

- With exposure, language seems to emerge naturally in children, suggesting humans have a biological predisposition for **language acquisition**.

- **Telegraphic speech**, errors of **overgeneralization** and **The Wug Test** all indicate that young children begin to understand and apply grammatical rules without explicit instruction.

- Acquisition of one's first language depends on early exposure and a **critical period** for proper language development means that exposure must happen before some time around age 7.

- While language doesn't determine thought (the **linguistic relativity hypothesis**), there is some evidence for ways that language may shape thought and perception.

- We are all subject to a number of **biases** which can distort our thinking including **overconfidence**, the **Wobegon Effect**, and **belief perseverance**.

- Rather than always using **algorithms** to solve problems, our brains seem to prefer using **heuristics**; mental shortcuts which allow us to make decisions quickly, though they also increase our risk of making errors.

Notes

Chapter 4
States of Consciousness

What is Consciousness?

Before we can consider different states of consciousness, we have to attempt an answer to a rather prickly question – What is consciousness? As we consider this question, we'll see a number of problems with even attempting to come up with answers.

The Mind-Body Problem

In Volume 1 we looked at Descartes' notion that the mind and body were separate entities. Descartes suggested that the non-material mind controlled the material body via the pineal gland, but as we'll see later in this chapter, the pineal gland is now known to serve other functions.

We may admit, however, that the mind does feel separate from the body. When we imagine ourselves looking out into the world, we may have a tendency to think in terms of the *Cartesian Theater*. This is the feeling that the mind is like a person inside of the head looking out at the world and controlling the body. This little person in the head doesn't really exist, of course, and if it were to exist, we would have to wonder what was inside of the head of that person inside the head, ad infinitum. This difficulty in understanding the relationship between the mind and the body is known as the *mind-body problem of consciousness*.

Zombie Apocalypse?

If I begin by at least accepting the notion that I'm conscious, how do I know that you are conscious? How can I be sure that I am not the only conscious one? In imagining a world in which no one else is actually conscious, you may realize that it might not be all that different from the world you currently experience. People move around, talk, and go to work and school, but what if they were all just automatons? What if they were just mindless zombies going about tasks with no internal mental experience at all? Sure, they could tell you they have internal experiences, but how could you be certain that their words weren't just for show, a clever ruse to throw you off track?

Certainly I could program a computer to say things that would make it sound like the computer has internal experience, but that wouldn't mean that it feels like something to be that computer. It seems that we naturally assume that other humans all have an internal mental experience, but can we ever really know?

This **problem of other minds** may make us wonder about the experience of other non-human organisms as well. In a famous essay, "What is it like to be a bat?" philosopher Thomas Nagel pondered this question. When we observe a bat's behavior, we might think there is "something it is like to be that organism" and then wonder what that something is actually like.

Nagel theorized, however, that it would be impossible for us to ever truly understand the experience of being a bat, because we are trapped in the viewpoint of being human. Nagel wrote that when he considers the experience of being a bat, "it tells me only what it would be like for me to behave as a bat does". Our assumptions and expectations of what it's like to be another animal probably reveal more about what it's like to be a human. So when you try to see the world through your dog's eyes, you reveal how you think dogs experience the world, which may not represent how dogs actually experience it. In attempting to imagine the experience of other minds, we cannot escape the experience of our own minds.

Perhaps even our tendency to imagine that others have internal mental experience is unique to our human minds. We seem to automatically assume internal intentions, characteristics, and traits simply by observing behavior. We do this when we observe other humans (which is why movies are more engrossing than just patterns of light on a screen) and also when we observe other animals and even objects. This was demonstrated in a classic study by Fritz Heider and Marianne Simmel in which participants observed a brief animation of two circles and a triangle moving around a square. After viewing the video, participants felt that the shapes had distinct personalities, motivations, and emotions. While this film certainly wouldn't win any Academy Awards, it demonstrates our human tendency to assume internal experience based solely on observation of behavior.

A Spectrum of Consciousness

In considering the consciousness of others, we might think of being conscious as being able to react to stimuli in the environment. This can be referred to as **minimal consciousness**. Of course, this minimal consciousness doesn't necessarily imply an experience of being that organism. Plants respond to light in their environment (and many even move toward it) but we may still doubt whether it feels like something to be a tree or a vine. On the other end of the spectrum, we might consider the rich and varied experience of full human consciousness, which includes responding to our environment as well as our own internal thoughts.

Part of the richness of this experience includes the ability to be aware of our own conscious processes and reflect on our own experience, known as ***self-consciousness***. In this way, we're able to make ourselves the object of our conscious focus (rather than just being the subject that is experiencing consciousness). We can consider how others view us and even reflect on our own thoughts and reflections.

Speaking of reflecting, one way of attempting to determine whether other animals have a sense of self-awareness is the ***mark test*** used by Gordon Gallup in 1970. After giving chimps some experience with mirrors, Gallup secretly placed a spot of dye on their faces, then had those chimps interact with a mirror again. If, upon seeing the spot, they reached toward their own faces, Gallup believed this indicated that they understood how mirrors worked and could view themselves as objects.

Other research has indicated that human children are able to pass this test by the age of about 18 months. This test has been repeated in a number of animal designs, revealing that humans are in select company when it comes to being able to recognize ourselves in mirrors. Other primates like chimps and orangutans are able to pass the test (along with elephants, dolphins, and perhaps some bird species) while most other animals fail. This may not come as a surprise to dog or cat owners who see their pets repeatedly flummoxed by mirrors, never learning that they are looking at their own reflections.

Of course, while it's certainly interesting to consider which animals seem to be able to recognize themselves, we still can't be sure that passing this test really reflects some special type of self-awareness.

What Purpose Does Consciousness Serve?

Even if I put aside the possibility that everyone else is a philosophical zombie and instead I assume that they do indeed have conscious experience, one large problem remains. If we aren't all zombies, why not? Why aren't we simply automatons? Why is there a subjective component to our experiences? And if we adopt a monist approach, how is it that this subjective experience arises from physical processes in the brain? This is known as the ***hard problem of consciousness***. And given just how hard a problem it is, we don't quite have a good answer for it. We may assume that there must be some sort of evolutionary advantages to developing consciousness, but it's hard to say for sure why those advantages couldn't arise in non-conscious zombies who were simply programmed to behave as we do.

Levels of Consciousness

Information in our minds may fall into a number of different categories of consciousness, depending on our level of access to the information. The ***conscious*** level contains information that we are presently aware of. This would include all the thoughts and sensations that we are currently thinking about. Thoughts that aren't in our conscious mind at the moment but can be brought into consciousness rather easily are considered to be at the ***preconscious*** level.

The ***subconscious*** level consists of influences and mental processes that we are generally unaware of, though we can see their effects on our behavior. We may not be aware of these in the moment, but we can clearly see how they have influenced behavior after the fact. This level would also include the subtle influence of priming and mere-exposure effects, which will be discussed later in this chapter (you can remember **sub**tle and **sub**conscious).

Things can get murky here because these subconscious influences are frequently described using the term ***unconscious***, though this is not meant to imply the Freudian/Psychodynamic unconscious. The Freudian ***unconscious*** level refers to wishes, desires, and fears which are repressed from the conscious mind in order to reduce anxiety, though the existence of this level of consciousness is disputed and not common in psychological research today.

Finally, the ***nonconscious*** level would include things that we are almost never aware of. This would include many processes of the autonomic nervous system such as muscle contractions for heart-rate or digestion, or levels of activation in different brain areas. We simply don't have conscious access to these processes in our body even if we try to think about them.

Consciousness During Waking Life

Even if we can't quite address all the philosophical questions that consciousness raises we can still consider what our subjective experience of consciousness is like and try to understand it. So let's consider some of the traits that consciousness seems to have (though there is still disagreement on some of these) as well as some evidence supporting the existence of these traits.

Unity – Consciousness is generally singular. While our precise state of consciousness may change, it tends to be considered a single state, rather than multiple consciousnesses at once. In this way, our consciousness tends toward unity. Consider watching a movie and you'll realize that we automatically incorporate the sights, sounds, and emotions into a single consciousness, rather than experiencing them as separate entities.

Intentionality – Intentionality means that consciousness is always focused on something. Consciousness seems to always be directed toward particular objects, thoughts, or events. Even when we daydream and our minds are wandering, in each moment our consciousness seems to be focused on something, whether that something is an internal thought, a particular sensation, or an external stimulus.

Selectivity – Our consciousness seems to be selective. It is able to pick up some messages and perceptions while ignoring others. This can be seen in what's known as the ***Cocktail Party Phenomenon***. Imagine that you are at a cocktail party, in a large room with a few dozen other people. People gather in clusters and there is the constant din of other conversations around you. In this situation, you are able to focus your attention on the particular conversation you are in, and everything else fades into a kind of background static.

It's not simply the case that you can't hear the others; it's that your attention is not directed toward them. In fact, if you were to eavesdrop on the conversation next to you, you might be able to hear it just fine. Now, without anything in the environment changing, your attention has selectively been placed on this other conversation, and the one you were previously in becomes background noise. We don't always have complete control of this selection process, however, as you've experienced if you've ever been in a conversation but then became distracted by hearing your name on the other side of the room. This cue can grab your attention and pull it to the other conversation. Hopefully you'll manage to switch your attention back to your present conversation before your partner asks a question, only to discover that you haven't really been listening.

This selective nature of attention can be tested in the laboratory in what's known as a **dichotic listening task**. In this design, participants attempt to listen to two messages simultaneously, one in each ear. Participants are asked to shadow one message by verbally repeating it. This ensures that their attention is focused on that message. When asked questions about the other message, however, participants show very little knowledge of it. In fact, they may not even notice if the voice of the other message changed or if the message was actually an incoherent jumble of words.

This type of research points out that we are not particularly good multi-taskers. Our attention doesn't divide well. So while you might occasionally manage to eavesdrop without getting caught, if you think you can text and drive you are wrong. You can drive, then text, then switch your attention back to driving, but you can't actually direct your attention to both activities at once. So while you may think you are skilled enough to multi-task (remember *illusory superiority*) the truth is that attention doesn't work that way. If you text and drive you put the safety of yourself and others at risk.

Our tiny spotlight of attention is actually much smaller than we think and anything going on outside of it is barely detected, if it is detected at all. This can be clearly seen in demonstrations of **change blindness**. In these studies, large changes can be made in the environment without people noticing, provided that their attention is directed elsewhere. In one clever study by Daniel Simons and Daniel Levin, a pedestrian asking for directions from a stranger was switched to a completely different person and in half of the trials the stranger didn't seem to notice the change.

A related phenomenon is ***inattentional blindness***, where we fail to detect an otherwise-obvious stimulus because our attention is directed elsewhere. This has also been demonstrated in studies by Simons and Christopher Chabris including a particularly well-known example involving basketball players. I don't want to give it away here (though perhaps I've said too much already) so I encourage you to check YouTube now for "the awareness test" and see just how well you can track the basketball players passing the ball.

SPOILER ALERT

Don't keep reading if you want to check your awareness in the Simons and Chabris demonstration. If you're already seen it or just watched it now, you may have missed (like more than half of the participants) the gorilla walking into the scene, beating his chest, then walking off. While your spotlight of attention was focused on the ball-passing by the white-shirted players, your mind filtered out the black-shirted players and as a result, inadvertently filtered out the gorilla costume as well. ****END SPOILER****

Transience – Finally, our minds love to wander. William James compared consciousness to a stream, because it was always moving and flowing. Our minds are constantly flitting about, moving from sights to sounds and feelings to thoughts, sampling widely from the surfeit of possible stimulation.

To remember these 4 traits of consciousness – ***unity, intentionality, selectivity***, and ***transience***, imagine that you are moving through a cave in the dark with a single flashlight. Now imagine that the spot of light from this flashlight represents your consciousness. There is only one spot of light (***unity***) it is always shining on something (***intentionality***), you have some control over where you point it (***selectivity***) and you'll have a tendency to keep moving it as you explore the cave (***transience***).

How Much Control Do We Have?

We may wonder just how much we control our own consciousness. For a brief demonstration of the problem of mental control, I can simply challenge you not to think of a white bear for the next 5 minutes. In a study by Daniel Wegner, participants given this thought-suppression challenge thought of white bears far more frequently than participants who were not told to suppress thoughts of white bears. This as an example of an ***ironic process of mental control***, in which our attempt to control our thoughts creates a counterintentional effect.

In addition to failures of conscious control, we may not realize that we've already ceded a great deal of control to unconscious processes. Even though our conscious attention tends toward unity, we also have subconscious processing that is occurring in parallel. This idea of simultaneous conscious and unconscious processing is known as **Dual-Process Theory** and it is often said we have a two-track mind: one track following our conscious experience, while the other track discreetly collects and processes information beneath our awareness. These tracks are also sometimes referred to as **System 1** (unconscious) and **System 2** (conscious). One way of getting a glimpse at the unconscious processing of System 1 is a technique known as **priming**.

Priming refers to how subtle cues in our environment can activate certain mental concepts which are then capable of influencing behavior. For a simple example, I could prime you by talking about sports, then ask you to quickly fill in the blanks below to create a word:

$$\_ \ \_ \ \text{L} \ \ \text{L}$$

You might come up with "ball", but if I had previously mentioned shopping you might be more likely to fill in the blanks to create "mall".

One of the most famous studies of priming, conducted by John Bargh and colleagues in 1996, involved priming participants for the concept of "elderly" by having them create sentences from scrambled words. For the experimental group, some sentences included terms like "Florida", "wrinkle", and "bingo", while controls completed the same task with non-age related terms. Bargh and colleagues then secretly recorded the time it took participants to walk to the elevator after the task and found that the elderly-primed participants walked more slowly than the controls. This suggests that subtle cues in our environment can have measurable impact on our behavior, though this influence may be outside of our conscious awareness.

Another unconscious influence on our behavior is the **mere-exposure effect**, which is that we have a tendency to like things more when they are more familiar to us. While this relationship between familiarity and fondness isn't exactly shocking, it may surprise you that this relationship holds even when people aren't aware of being exposed to the stimulus. Research by Robert Zajonc (pronounced like "science" but starting with a "z") and colleagues found that Chinese characters repeatedly flashed on a screen too quickly for conscious awareness were later rated as more likeable than other characters by participants who couldn't read Chinese. Similar effects of repeated exposure have been found for nonsense words, tones, and even people's faces.

Advertisers are acutely aware of the effect of familiarity, and as a result they spend millions of dollars getting products in front of our faces. Most people insist that ads don't affect their behavior, but this is probably because some of the effects are occurring unconsciously. It's not that you see an advertisement and immediately run to the store, but rather that you may unconsciously develop greater fondness for that particular brand because you have seen it before.

Of course, the effects of priming and mere-exposure are subtle and it seems that environments must be carefully controlled in order to observe them. They certainly shouldn't be seen as magical brain-washing or powerful subliminal mind-control techniques. Nevertheless, they should make us question just how much we control our conscious behavior and how much influence is exerted outside of our conscious awareness.

Consciousness During Sleeping Life

You may think, as many people do, that sleeping is a type of unconsciousness, but this isn't accurate. Despite expressions like "dead to the world", sleepers do have some awareness of their surroundings. They manage to keep their bodies in their beds, and in the case of dreaming, they certainly have a vivid experience of being asleep. In fact, stimuli from a sleeper's environment may even be seamlessly incorporated into dreams, which you may have experienced if the sound of your alarm clock has ever found its way into your dreams as a blaring fire alarm, a ringing phone, or a singing banana.

So rather than unconsciousness, we should think of sleeping as another state of consciousness that differs from waking life. Instead of sleep and wakefulness as an on/off switch for consciousness, we should think of a dimmer switch, which allows us to slide back and forth between different levels of awareness.

The Rhythm of the Night

Our sleeping pattern follows a ***circadian rhythm***, which is really just a way of saying a daily pattern of wakefulness and sleepiness (circadian derived from Latin: *circa* - "about" and *diem* - "day"). Our circadian rhythm is influenced by environmental factors, known as ***zeitgebers*** (German for "time-givers") which help to set this internal clock.

One of the most most powerful zeitgebers is light. When light hits your retina, messages are not only sent to the occipital lobe for visual processing, they are also sent to the *suprachiasmatic nucleus*, an area of the hypothalamus. In the presence of light (especially wavelengths corresponding to blue light), the suprachiasmatic nucleus inhibits the *pineal gland* from releasing melatonin into the bloodstream. *Melatonin* is a hormone which, when released into the bloodstream, causes us to feel drowsy. Through this process of inhibiting melatonin release, light helps to keep us feeling alert, while darkness helps bring drowsiness.

This process probably worked quite well in setting our circadian rhythm for millions of years of our evolutionary history, but the ubiquity of artificial light in most of our lives today may be interrupting this system. While our ancestors only really had bright light from the sun, we can have bright light any time we want. The darkness of dusk that told our ancestors to unwind and stay in the safety of shelter now simply signals us to turn on the lights.

If you have trouble falling asleep at night, light may be part of the problem and limiting your exposure to it in the evening may help you to fall asleep more easily. You may even consider using blue-light blocking glasses in the evening or downloading programs like f.lux which reduce the amount of blue-light emitted by your laptop or phone screen after sunset.

Light is not the only zeitgeber that influences our level of alertness. The timing of our meals, the ambient temperature, and our social interactions also play a role in the circadian rhythm. This may explain how you managed to stay awake all night at slumber parties and why it's so easy to fall asleep in a warm room while a lecturer drones on and on without any chance of interaction.

The settings of this internal clock also vary with age, as teenagers tend to be "night-owls" whose concentration and attention peak later in the day or evening, while older adults tend to be "larks" who perform best in early morning, then decline as the hours go by. This is clearly seen in the classic class-time conundrum, as adults (parents and teachers) set the times that work best for them, while teenagers are alert at 11pm but stumbling and slumbering through early morning classes.

The Sleep Cycle

As we sleep through any given night, we move through a number of different stages of sleep. These different stages can be identified by their differing patterns of brain activity, as recorded by an **EEG** (*electroencephalogram*). These measurements of electrical activity in the brain are recorded in the form of waves, with peak and valleys, and the resulting patterns are where we get the term "brain waves". In an awake but relaxed, drowsy, or meditative state, the brain produces "**alpha waves**", while a state of vigilance produces "**beta waves**".

When we first fall asleep, we move through the following stages of sleep. The first 3 stages are referred to as NREM, for Non-Rapid-Eye-Movement sleep.

NREM Stage 1 – Stage 1 is characterized by de-synchronized **theta waves**; slow irregular waves of activity. In this stage, sleepers may experience brief dream-like visions, known as *hypnagogic imagery*, and occasionally experience sudden twitches and falling sensations, known as *hypnic jerks*. This stage may last for only a few minutes before moving to stage 2.

NREM Stage 2 – Theta waves continue, though occasionally interrupted by sudden bursts of activity, known as **sleep spindles**. In this stage we also see high amplitude spikes known as **K-complexes**, which are hypothesized to reduce cortical arousal and help maintain sleep. When you first fall asleep, this stage will generally last for around 15-20 minutes. Throughout the course of a night, about 50% of sleep time will be spent in Stage 2 sleep.

NREM Stage 3 – By stage 3 we see more obvious changes in brain activity as the waves increase their amplitude and decrease their frequency while also becoming more synchronized, resulting in "**delta waves**". This stage is considered to be the stage of deepest sleep and lowest awareness of surroundings. If you're groggy and confused when someone wakes you (known as *sleep inertia*), there's a good chance that you were in this "slow-wave" sleep at the time. Note: you may see reference to Stage 4 sleep in some texts; the American Academy of Sleep Medicine reclassified the stages in 2007, combining stage 3 and 4 into a single stage.

So far this probably seems as you'd expect; the longer you've been asleep, the deeper the level of sleep. But after about an hour, something bizarre happens. The depth of your sleep lessens as you rise back up to stage 2, and then you enter the most interesting stage of all.

REM Sleep

REM sleep or *rapid-eye-movement sleep*, is sometimes referred to as *paradoxical sleep*, and with good reason. In contrast to the other stages, in REM heart rate, blood pressure, and respiration increase, along with physical signs of sexual arousal. Every 30 seconds or so your eyes begin moving around under your eyelids (hence the name). Your brain activity closely resembles that of a waking state, and yet your body becomes paralyzed. People who are awakened from Non-REM stages may report some dreamlike imagery, but those awakened from REM report vivid dreaming.

Who Needs Sleep?

Although the processes of sleep are not yet fully understood, REM seems to be particularly important for the consolidation of memory. The importance of REM can be seen in the fact that people (and animals) who are temporarily deprived of REM sleep for a night will experience a *rebound effect*; spending more time in REM than usual during subsequent sleep. Babies spend more time in REM than adults, and people who are experiencing higher levels of stress will also spend more time in REM when they sleep.

For most people, an entire sleep cycle from Stage 1 to a completed period of REM will last about 90 minutes. At this point the cycle is repeated, though in subsequent cycles we spend less time in deep sleep (by the end of the night skipping slow-wave sleep completely) and spend more time in REM sleep. While initial REM stages may last for 15 or 20 minutes, later cycles may have REM sessions lasting 45 minutes to an hour.

One way of assessing the importance of sleep is to consider what happens when we don't get it. This can be considered either by examining the effects of *chronic sleep deprivation*, in which people are repeatedly not getting enough sleep, or by *acute sleep deprivation*, in which people stay awake continuously.

Physical effects of Sleep Deprivation

Sleep deprivation causes a number of physical changes in the body. Physical symptoms of sleep deprivation include fatigue, dark circles and/or bags under the eyes (caused by the very thin layers of skin in this area becoming more pale and allowing blood vessels to become more visible), fluctuations in hormone levels, and reduced performance on physical tasks.

Chronic sleep deprivation is associated with obesity, which may be a result of several hormonal changes which occur during sleep deprivation. Going without enough sleep increases levels of the hormone ghrelin, which increases feelings of hunger, and deprivation decreases the hormone leptin, which helps to signal satiety. As a result, sleep-deprived people are more likely to have cravings for food and also likely to eat more before feeling full. Sleep deprivation also reduces willpower, which means that when those cravings hit they may be even harder to resist.

Sleep deprivation also increases levels of the stress hormone cortisol, which can trigger the body to store fat. This stress response also means that sleep deprivation suppresses the activity of the immune system. This means that people who don't get enough sleep are more likely to get sick, and also explains why when we do get sick we tend to spend more time asleep (in order to activate the immune system).

Cognitive Effects of Sleep Deprivation

Sleep deprivation has profound effects on cognition and attention. Both chronic and acute sleep deprivation impair concentration, memory, judgment, coordination, and reaction time. These cognitive deficits shouldn't just concern you when it comes to your exam performance after an all-nighter. The potential for serious injury and death from sleep deprivation is high. Studies of "drowsy driving" have found impairments similar to drunk driving and driver fatigue has been estimated to be responsible for 100,000 crashes, 1,550 deaths and 71,000 injuries every year in the United States alone. So even if you join Edgar Allan Poe in loathing sleep as "little slices of death", remember that trying to do without sleep may lead to a death far more permanent.

Sleep Disorders

The most common sleep disorder is ***insomnia***, and it is estimated that about 10% of adults will suffer from insomnia at some point in their lifetime. Insomnia is a persistent difficulty or inability to enter the sleep state, or to remain asleep, often despite feeling tired. So while we all occasionally have difficulty getting to sleep at night, in most cases this wouldn't be considered to be clinical insomnia.

While you may think that sleeping pills (or an alcoholic "night-cap") would help those with insomnia, these aren't recommended. While sleeping pills may aid muscle relaxation or reduce anxiety to help patients enter the sleep state, unfortunately they reduce the quality of REM sleep. This means that while patients may spend more time sleeping, they end up getting less REM sleep and as a result still feel tired.

Insomnia sufferers also have a tendency to underestimate how much sleep they are getting, often believing they are sleeping half as much as they actually are. This may occur because they enter the sleep state and reawaken without realizing they were actually asleep. If they repeatedly check the clock throughout the night they may think that they were awake until 2 or 3am, when some of that time was spent asleep. They may also recall waking during the night and believe that they stayed awake much longer than they actually did.

Another common sleep disorder affecting about 5% of people (though more common in males) is **sleep apnea**. In this disorder, when muscles in the throat relax during sleep, the tongue and epiglottis obstruct the flow of air. This is also what causes those strange sounds of snoring, except in sleep apnea airflow is completely blocked. This blockage of airflow causes the patient to awaken in order to breathe. Patients with sleep apnea may not remember awakening throughout the night, but report feeling tired and lethargic despite what appears to be adequate sleeping time.

Obesity increases the risk of sleep apnea, though as we've seen already, sleep deprivation (which would be a side effect of sleep apnea) also increases the risk of obesity, so this interaction could be working both ways. A common treatment for sleep apnea is to use a CPAP (continuous positive airway pressure) machine. This device consists of a mask, worn at night, which slightly increases air pressure on the throat, helping to keep the airway open and allowing the patient to remain breathing (and sleeping).

Sleep walking (or *somnambulism*) occurs during the deep stages of slow-wave sleep. The sleeper may get out of bed, wander around, and even eat or perform other behaviors while still in the sleep state. Sleep walking is more common in young children, especially males, and often goes away on its own by adolescence. Episodes of sleepwalking and behaviors performed are rarely recalled the next morning.

Children are also more likely than adults to suffer from **night terrors**. In night terrors, the person wakes up in the middle of the night and may scream, feeling an overwhelming sense of fear, and usually doesn't remember the experience in the morning. Like sleepwalking, night terrors also tend to fade by the end of childhood.

REM Sleep Behavior disorder is a rare disorder in which the usual paralysis and loss of muscle tone (*muscle atonia*) of REM sleep does not occur. This means that sufferers are able to engage in "dream enactment", which can have dangerous consequences. They may kick, punch, scream, or jump out of bed, potentially injuring themselves or their bed partner. REM sleep behavior disorder can be treated with muscle relaxants to reduce activity, in addition to creating a safer environment for the sleeper which may even include a special sleeping bag that helps to restrict movements.

Narcolepsy is a rare sleep disorder affecting about 1 in 2000 people (0.05%), in which patients suffer from an irrepressible need to sleep, even though they are spending adequate amounts of time sleeping at night. They repeatedly lapse into sleep and often also experience *cataplexy*, a sudden loss of muscle tone. The sudden attacks of sleep generally only last for a few minutes and may occur at any time, making it difficult for sufferers of narcolepsy to live a normal life. Narcolepsy sufferers tend to enter the REM state very quickly after falling asleep, meaning that they spend less time in slow-wave stages of sleep, which may relate to their feelings of drowsiness during the day.

Narcolepsy can be treated with stimulants (such as *Modafinil)* which promote wakefulness, though these do not cure the disorder. Some sufferers remain awake and aware of their surroundings during *cataplexy* but are unable to move. People nearby may attempt to "awaken" the person with pinches or shouting. The sufferer can feel and hear these attempts but is unable to respond.

Polyphasic Sleep Schedules

You may have heard of polyphasic sleeping schedules, which involve splitting sleep time up into several separate chunks throughout a 24 hour period. Attempts to adopt these schedules seem to be spurred by claims from Thomas Edison that sleep is a "complete waste of time" and they are encouraged by life-hackers seeking to supposedly maximize sleep efficiency. These schedules are often claimed to derive from the odd sleeping habits of eminent thinkers like Leonardo DaVinci and Nikola Tesla, though evidence that these figures actually followed these types of schedules for extended periods is scant to nonexistent.

We should note that much of the initial research on polyphasic schedules conducted by Claudio Stampi was intended to determine sleep efficiency in a particular subset of people: solo-sailors during lengthy competitions in which full periods of sleep were not possible. Stampi tested a number of possible ways of dividing sleep in order to assess which allowed for greater physical performance over a relatively short period of time. Life-hackers tend to ignore that these schedules weren't intended to be adopted as routine sleeping habits, but were for specific short-term situations which necessitated some level of chronic sleep deprivation.

We should also avoid thinking that just because there are names for these schedules this means they are actually viable ways of organizing quality sleep. Unfortunately creating names like the "Everyman" and "Uberman" schedule may give a false sense of credibility to these schedules. This is related to a cognitive error known as the *nominal fallacy*, which is the flaw of thinking that because we have a name for something we actually understand it. So if I were to invent the "Deca-doze Distribution" of sleeping for 10 minutes every 2 hours the mere fact that I've given it a scientific-sounding name might make people more likely to believe it's something that can be done.

You should also note that in evolutionary terms these schedules don't make much sense. We have evolved to be alert and awake during the day (when we can hunt and gather) and sleep during the night (when it's dark and we are more vulnerable). This rhythm indicates that we are best suited to a single long session of sleep (*monophasic*) or perhaps a *biphasic schedule*, which is a large chunk of sleep at night, with the addition of an early afternoon siesta. Attempting to drastically deviate from the circadian rhythm which has developed over millions of years seems unlikely to create benefits, and as we've already seen, the risks of sleep deprivation are great.

So if you've been tempted to try adopting one of these polyphasic schedules, remember that sleeping less in exchange for more grogginess, irritability, cognitive deficits, and a higher risk of fatality from accidents doesn't seem like a particularly wise trade-off. There's a certain irony to the belief that if you want to be successful and productive you need to learn how to sleep less. In actuality, achieving high levels of performance, in both cognitive and physical tasks, seems to necessitate spending more time in sleep. Sleep helps to consolidate new memories, enhance concentration, and improve reaction time, endurance, mood, and energy levels. So ignore those admonitions from Edison and help uncover your potential by spending more time under the covers.

Theories of Dreaming

Freud's approach to understanding dreaming was based on the assumption that dreams were representations of unconscious desires. Because these desires are too anxiety-producing for us to consciously consider, they are not directly revealed. One way they emerge, according to Freud, is when we are dreaming.

He believed that dreams consisted of two features, the manifest content and the latent content. The ***manifest content*** is what we are shown, meaning what we actually dream about. So if we dream about riding a train, arguing with a talking dolphin, or watching a burning tree, these would be the manifest content.

The ***latent content***, however, is the hidden message behind the dream. It's those anxiety-producing unconscious fears and desires that our conscious mind needs to be shielded from. So our dream about a train may be about sex, the dolphin might represent conflict with our mother, or the burning tree the death of a friend. Freud believed that a therapist could analyze the manifest content of a patient's dreams and, over time, uncover clues about the unconscious forces shaping the patient's personality.

There are two main problems with this approach to understanding dreams. The first is that we frequently dream explicitly about our desires and fears. These often manifest themselves quite directly in dreams and we have conscious access to these themes. We actually do dream of having sex, fighting with a parent, losing a friend, or any number of other stressful and anxiety-producing events. If these desires must be hidden from consciousness, why would they sometimes appear in the manifest content?

Secondly, there are infinite possible interpretations of the manifest content, so we can never be sure which interpretation is correct. What your therapist thinks a train or a dolphin means may actually reveal more about the therapist's mind than it reveals about your own.

So while Freud's notion that there are hidden clues to the unconscious in dreams gained some popularity, it ultimately failed to provide a satisfying answer to why exactly we dream what we dream. It may be true that dreams reveal some aspects of our thoughts as well as our hopes, fears, and desires. What doesn't seem to be true is that these elements are revealed through predictable patterns and symbols.

A Brain-Based Approach

In 1977, J. Allan Hobson and Robert McCarley proposed a new theory of dreaming, ***the activation-synthesis model***. The activation-synthesis model suggests that during sleep, brain activation occurs somewhat randomly, and these patterns of random activation are combined and interpreted (synthesis) by the brain. This results in the bizarre (and characteristic) features of dreams. In this model, dreams are seen as the brain's flailing attempt to make sense of these unusual patterns of activation.

This approach attempts to explain the apparently inexplicable nature of dreams by suggesting that often our brains are dealing with patterns of activation that simply don't occur in waking life. The brain is being forced to come up with explanations for bizarre patterns of activity and we're just left watching the show (and scratching our heads as to what the director was thinking). If, for instance, you find yourself dreaming that you are now vacationing with your 3rd grade art teacher, it's probably not because of some repressed sexual desire (as a Freudian might suggest), but rather that your memory for that teacher just happened to be stimulated at the same time as your memory for last year's travels. In a valiant attempt to reconcile this new pattern, your ever-explaining brain creates a storyline in which the two coexist.

Information-Processing

Since the activation-synthesis model was first proposed, there has been considerably more research on the patterns of activation that occur during REM sleep, suggesting that perhaps the activation isn't quite random. This ***information-processing dream theory*** considers that the activation patterns that occur during REM serve other purposes and are not simply random noise. Neural activation in dreaming may allow our brains to sift through new experiences, revisit old memories, and maintain neural connections and networks.

One way that this can be seen is in how our dreams often incorporate "day residue" of our present situations and experiences, combined with memories from years or even decades before. If we spend hours playing a video game during the day, imagery from the game tends to show up in dreams that night but may be combined with other memories or situations.

If, as Robert Stickgold has suggested, one role of sleep is to consolidate memories and integrate our experiences into a cohesive sense of self, it may no longer come as a surprise that dreams combine our recent experiences and learning with other memories. Rather than random activation, this may reflect sleep's role in reorganizing information and considering alternatives in order to inform our future responses.

This might also account for common themes in dreams, as we all share many similar problems, fears (predators or exams), sources of embarrassment (oops I forgot my pants), or worries for the future (I've lost my teeth and hair) that our minds are simulating and working out responses to. At the same time, it accounts for individual differences, as how our brains choose to interpret, explain, and react to these simulations may reflect something of our own unique experiences and viewpoints.

Finally, a section on dreaming wouldn't be complete without mentioning *lucid dreaming*. Lucid dreaming is when a dreamer becomes aware of the dream state, but remains asleep. The dreamer may then be able to take conscious control of the dream and direct the course of events. This raises some questions about the nature of consciousness during dreaming and how awareness that one is dreaming may be separated from the dream experience itself. Stephen LaBerge has spent decades studying lucid dreaming and believes that anyone can learn to lucid dream on a regular basis. He has written several books on learning to lucid dream and believes that lucid dreaming can help to foster greater creativity, insight, and new perspectives and interpretations of events and behaviors.

Drugs and Consciousness

In Volume 1 we looked at several drug and neurotransmitter interactions such as nicotine and acetylcholine, and alcohol and GABA, to understand how chemical interactions in the brain influence behavior. What we didn't address, however, is how these might influence our consciousness. In this section, we'll look at how *psychoactive drugs*, substances which alter the chemistry of the brain, are capable of altering our state of consciousness.

Getting Into the Brain

Generally speaking, the brain doesn't want to be messed with, so to keep things under control, the **blood-brain barrier** prevents most things in the bloodstream from getting into the brain. This blood-brain barrier works by only allowing certain molecules, like vital nutrients, through its special channels. This is generally a good thing, and why brain viruses and infections are so rare. Even if an infection is in your body and traveling in your bloodstream, the tight-knit endothelial cells of the blood-brain barrier can usually provide an adequate security network. The downside is that when you do have an infection in your brain, it's especially difficult to get medication in to fight it.

Some chemicals, however, are able to sneak through this barrier, gain access to the brain, and influence its functioning. Once inside the brain, these chemicals can travel to synapses and affect neural communication. Some chemicals boost the message of a neurotransmitter, either by mimicking the action of the neurotransmitter, blocking its removal from the synapse, or stimulating its release. These drugs are considered to be **agonists** for the neurotransmitter they influence. Other drugs, however, do the opposite and decrease the effects of a neurotransmitter by blocking its receptor sites, increasing its removal, or decreasing its release. These drugs are **antagonists** for the neurotransmitter affected.

This agonist/antagonist categorization doesn't address the effects the drugs have on behavior or cognition. Based on their effects, drugs can be roughly categorized into 3 main groups: **depressants**, **stimulants**, or **hallucinogens**. Of course, because it's possible to influence more than one neurotransmitter or more than one brain area or body function, some drugs may fit into more than one category.

In considering the effects of these different types of drugs, we should remember that the body is constantly trying to maintain a state of **homeostasis**, the balance needed to maintain normal functioning. Repeated introduction of drugs into the brain causes changes, known as **neuroadaptation**. This is how **tolerance** to a drug builds over time. After repeated exposure, the brain builds a resistance to the effects of the drug, so a greater dosage is required to achieve the same effects, perhaps explaining why just one cup of coffee doesn't get you going like it used to.

After a tolerance has developed, neuroadaptation also explains why going without the drug can be difficult. This is known as **withdrawal**. Essentially the brain has adapted to having the drug around, and has developed a **dependence** on the drug's effects. In the case of caffeine, sudden cessation may result in a minor headache, but for more powerful drugs, withdrawal can be an overwhelmingly painful experience. Intense cravings combined with physical pain can drive a user back to the drug, even though he may rationally know that it is destroying his life.

This **physical addiction** to the chemical reactions a drug causes is not the only type of addiction, and users may also experience **psychological addiction** to a substance. In this case, people believe they need the drug, or find using it to be a way of coping. Alcohol is a good example of a drug that is physically addictive but also has strong psychological components of addiction. People may feel a desire for alcohol in order to function in particular social situations or in order to deal with disappointment, stress, or anxiety. Even after the physical symptoms of withdrawal have faded, a former alcoholic may still have difficulty dealing with the psychological components of addiction in certain situations.

Stimulants

Stimulants are drugs which speed up processes in the body and stimulate the autonomic nervous system. These drugs increase heart rate, blood pressure, and breathing, and may increase our state of vigilance while decreasing feelings of tiredness. In addition to this stimulation, some stimulants activate the reward area of the hypothalamus, triggering a rush of dopamine that causes short-lived feelings of euphoria and well-being. Common stimulant drugs include caffeine (which is the world's most commonly used psychoactive drug), cocaine, amphetamines, methamphetamine, and ecstasy (MDMA – *methylenedioxymethamphetamine*).

Depressants

Depressants have the opposite effect on the nervous system, slowing processes and inhibiting activation. This causes slowed heart rate and breathing, and reduced muscle tension. Depressants include alcohol (specifically *ethanol*) and tranquilizers (also known as *anxiolytics* or anti-anxiety drugs) which include barbiturates and benzodiazepines (like Valium and Xanax).

Overdose of depressant drugs can lead to enough inhibition of function to induce a coma or even cause death. Withdrawal can also be dangerous, as the body's dependence on the inhibiting effects of regular use mean that sudden cessation can cause *excitotoxicity*. Dependency causes the nervous system to be overstimulated when the depressant drug is no longer suppressing function, causing anxiety, seizures, and in extreme cases, death.

Narcotics (including *Opiates*) are sometimes classified as a separate category of drugs but can be considered depressants because of their inhibiting effects on the nervous system. The word narcotics comes from the Greek root *narko* meaning "numbness" or "stupor". The term *narcotics* can be misleading though, as legal definitions differ from medical definitions. In the United States any prohibited drug may be referred to as a narcotic, so the term can refer to cocaine (a stimulant) and marijuana (a hallucinogen) even though in medical terms neither would be considered a narcotic.

In medical terms, narcotics are pain-relievers that mimic the body's own natural painkillers (*endorphins*) and include morphine, heroin, methadone, oxycodone, codeine, and opium (from which *opiates* and *opioids* get their name). These drugs block pain messages and provide a sense of euphoric, drowsy bliss for the user. Unfortunately, neuroadaptation occurs rapidly with opiates, causing the body to reduce endorphin production, thus leaving it unable to manage pain well on its own. Without natural endorphins to block their pain, recovering addicts face an agonizing withdrawal process where it can seem the only thing to stop their pain is the very drug they are trying to avoid. This torturous withdrawal process explains why these drugs can exert such a powerful influence over users.

Hallucinogens

The last category of psychoactive drugs includes those drugs which alter perception of reality and identity, and have the potential to induce sensory hallucinations. *Hallucinogens* (also known as *psychedelics*) include LSD (*lysergic acid diethylamide*), mescaline, psilocybin mushrooms, marijuana, PCP (*phencyclidine*), ketamine, and ecstasy (which is also a stimulant).

The effects of hallucinogenic drugs are considered to be less predictable than other drugs and seem to be more dependent on psychological factors such as the user's expectations and emotional state. Another difference from stimulants and depressants is that hallucinogens may remain in the body considerably longer. For instance, by-products of THC (*delta-9-tetrahydrocannabinol*) in marijuana may remain in the body as long as a month, and this lingering means that subsequent uses may actually have a stronger effect than the initial use. This may allow regular users to get high using a smaller dose of the drug and is referred to as ***reverse tolerance***.

With a few exceptions (like PCP and ketamine) the physical withdrawal and dependency seen in other drug types is not common with hallucinogenic drugs. While animals will press levers thousands of times to get another hit of coke or meth, they generally won't work to get hits of LSD or psilocybin. As a result, these drugs generally aren't considered to be physically addictive in the same way as heroin, cocaine, alcohol, or even caffeine.

This does not mean that addiction isn't possible, however, as psychological addiction may still occur, particularly if these drugs are used to escape negative emotions or stress. The fact that they don't tend to cause withdrawal also doesn't mean that they aren't harmful. There are still a number of negative effects associated with their use including anxiety, paranoia, and problems in learning and memory formation.

While all the drugs mentioned above have physiological effects on the body, expectancy and beliefs also influence how they affect consciousness. While this is especially true of hallucinogens, it's also true of other drug types. People can be duped into believing that decaf coffee has improved their alertness (if they don't know it was decaf) or that non-alcoholic beverages have made them tipsy. These effects of beliefs and expectations mean that drugs aren't the only ways of changing our state of consciousness and it has been suggested that hypnosis and meditation can also create altered states of consciousness.

Hypnosis

In considering what hypnosis is, perhaps we should start by considering what hypnosis is not. Despite what you may have seen in a stage show, on television, or in movies, hypnosis is not a magical state of mind-control in which a hypnotized subject obeys the every whim of the hypnotist. Instead, we can think of a hypnotic state as a state of relaxation, focused attention, and increased imagination. This state is generally entered via hypnotic induction, in which the hypnotist encourages the subject to become relaxed, then gradually makes suggestions to the subject (your eyelids are becoming heavier, your eyes are closing, etc.). People vary in how strongly they respond to these suggestions, and this is referred to as their ***hypnotic suggestibility***. Some people are considered to be "highly hypnotizable" and become absorbed in the suggestions of the hypnotist.

We shouldn't equate hypnotic suggestibility with mere gullibility, however, and when subjects are given this negative connotation their hypnotic suggestibility sharply decreases. We might think of hypnotic suggestibility as an ability to focus attention and imagination on the suggestions of the hypnotist. A sense of will remains, however, and subjects who have been hypnotized will not perform tasks that they would not otherwise do.

Therapeutic Uses of Hypnosis

The increased state of imagination and attention does allow some therapeutic use for hypnosis, the most prominent of which is pain reduction (*analgesia*). Subjects who are hypnotized may also have greater access to their own healing powers, which may be similar to the placebo effect. Hypnosis has been used to successfully treat stress-related skin problems, asthma, and obesity. Its use in treating addictions to alcohol, nicotine, and other drugs, however, has not been shown to be as successful.

Despite the popular perception, hypnosis is not able to increase accuracy of past memories. As we saw in chapter 2, our memory is subject to failures and biases, and unfortunately hypnosis is unable to overcome these. One thing it is able to do, however, is make subjects more confident in the accuracy of their memories, even though the memories are not actually more accurate. This can be a dangerous combination, particularly when these supposed recovered memories involve allegations of crime or abuse.

While it can't successfully recover repressed memories, hypnosis does seem to be able to reduce memories of the hypnotic session itself, known as ***posthypnotic amnesia***. Subjects can also engage in directed forgetting, in which they respond to suggestions that certain information or experiences will not be remembered following the session.

How does Hypnosis Happen?

One theory for explaining the behavior of hypnotized subjects is that they are like actors on a stage. They are obeying the hypnotist, who acts as a director and manages their perceptions. This is known as ***Role Theory of Hypnosis***, and if we accept this explanation, we might think that hypnosis is not in fact an altered state of consciousness.

Another theory, however, suggests that hypnosis really is a different state from normal wakefulness and involves a division of consciousness. This ***Dissociation Theory***, proposed by Ernest Hilgard, notes that hypnotized subjects may continue to follow suggestions even when they believe they are not being observed. This would indicate that hypnosis is more than just playing along. The fact the hypnosis can also effectively be used to manage pain suggests that it may actually be altering the perceptual experiences of subjects. Hilgard demonstrated this by asking hypnotized subjects to hold their hands in icy water. These subjects were then asked about whether they were experiencing pain. While subjects said they weren't experiencing pain, they still showed awareness that the icy water was actually painful. This suggested to Hilgard that the subjects were splitting their consciousness between awareness of the pain (which they had) and the experience of the pain (which was reduced).

Meditation

Another possible altered state of consciousness can be seen in meditation. In many ways, hypnosis and meditation are quite similar, as they both are a state of relaxed awareness, though meditation does not necessarily focus on particular suggestions. While there are many varieties and traditions of meditation, we will briefly focus on two types: focused awareness meditation and mindfulness meditation. Both of these practices involve cultivating a relaxed and calm state of mind.

In *focused attention meditation* the meditator chooses a single focus of attention and attempts to maintain this focus. The sole focus of attention may be one's breathing or it may be a *mantra*; a word or phrase that is repeated (mentally or chanted). While you may have heard of some of the familiar mantras like "Om" or "Hare Krishna" that are used by some groups, any word at all can be used. The importance of the mantra is to track one's awareness and notice when it has deviated.

Another type of meditation is *mindfulness meditation*. The main difference here is that rather than maintaining a single focus, the meditator attends to all the sights, sounds, feelings, and thoughts that occur, but without becoming attached to any of them. Jon Kabat-Zinn describes mindfulness as "paying attention in a particular way: on purpose, in the present moment, and nonjudgmentally".

There may be similarities here to the dissociation theory of hypnosis, where subjects seem to separate their awareness of sensations from their experience of those sensations. Experienced meditators engaging in mindfulness meditation have shown similar types of analgesia, having awareness of pain but having reduced experience and emotional reactivity to the pain.

Herbert Benson has researched how the practice of meditation elicits the "*relaxation response*" a metabolic change that activates the parasympathetic nervous system. This is essentially the opposite of the "fight or flight response". This relaxation response reduces activation of the sympathetic nervous system, decreasing heart rate, blood pressure, and stress hormones, while increasing relaxation, digestion, and immune function.

How to Start Practicing Meditation

While this isn't intended to be a comprehensive guide to meditation, I thought I would give readers a few pointers if they are interested in how to begin. Meditation isn't all that complicated, and all that you really need to do is set aside some time to sit quietly and calm your mind.

The first point that beginners may struggle with is the widespread misconception that meditation is some sort of esoteric and mystical experience. You don't need to understand how to balance your *qi*, align your *chakras*, or look out your third eye in order to meditate properly. You don't need to travel to Tibetan mountaintops or gaze at Ganesh under the guidance of a guru in order to get the calming benefits that meditation can give. While understanding these cultural traditions and practices can be fascinating, it's not a prerequisite for getting started.

Another problem that plagues people who want to start meditating is the feeling that they just can't do it. Their mind wanders, they feel uncomfortable or restless, and they give up, thinking that meditation is not for them. If you're looking to start regular meditation, remember that trying to maintain a single focus, getting distracted, then bringing your mind back to focus is what meditation is. It doesn't mean that you're doing it wrong or that it's not for you. Focus, distraction, and refocus are supposed to happen, so accept this cycle. Continuing to sit quietly and face down distraction and discomfort is a challenge, and that's exactly the point.

Choose a comfortable sitting posture (lying down usually leads to falling asleep, which is not what we want), choose something to focus on (your breathing, a mantra, or your present sensations), and you've begun to meditate. If you can embrace the fact that you aren't waiting for anything miraculous to happen and you recognize that catching your mind wandering is what meditation is, then you're on the right path toward cultivating this practice. Realizing that this is a practice that needs to be cultivated means you don't need to start with 45 minutes or an hour all at once. Start with a small goal that is attainable (maybe just 5 minutes per day) then gradually build as you get more comfortable with the practice.

While this is all you really need to get started, if you want to read more about meditation, I highly recommend the writing of Jon Kabat-Zinn, especially "Wherever You Go, There You Are" which was quoted above. His writing is clear, accessible, and inspiring, and is what has helped me most with meditation. I hope that you'll consider creating the habit of regular meditation and I wish you the best on this journey!

Chapter Summary – States of Consciousness

- The study of consciousness is wrought with problems including the ***mind-body problem***, the ***problem of other minds***, and the ***hard problem of consciousness***. Four characteristics that generally describe consciousness are ***unity***, ***intentionality***, ***selectivity***, and ***transience***.

- Our level of awareness of information can be classified as ***conscious***, ***preconscious***, ***subconscious*** (also ***unconscious***), or ***nonconscious***. Studies on ***priming*** and the ***mere-exposure effect*** support the existence of a separate track of subconscious processing, referred to as ***System 1*** in ***Dual-Process Theory***.

- The ***circadian rhythm*** refers to our "internal clock" or pattern of alertness throughout the day and is influenced by ***zeitgebers*** such as exposure to light, meal times, and social interaction.

- The sleep cycle is divided into 4 stages; NREM 1, NREM 2, NREM 3, and REM sleep. Proper sleep may be disrupted by a number of disorders including ***insomnia***, ***sleep apnea***, ***sleepwalking***, ***night terrors***, ***REM sleep behavior disorder***, and ***narcolepsy***.

- Depending on how they alter the nervous system and consciousness, ***psychoactive drugs*** can be categorized as ***stimulants***, ***depressants***, or ***hallucinogens***.

- ***Hypnosis*** is a state of increased imagination and suggestibility which can be used to treat some illnesses and reduce pain. ***Meditation*** is a state of relaxed awareness which can also reduce the experience of pain and activate the parasympathetic nervous system.

Notes

Thanks for Reading!

Congratulations for making it through this rather dense guide. I hope that it has helped you to have a better grasp of these concepts. I encourage you check out the free resources at **www.psychexamreview.com!**

In the pages that follow you'll find lists of key terms, as well as references and recommended readings for each chapter. Thanks again for reading, and I wish you all the best in your study of psychology!

Learning – Key Terms

learning

behaviorism

classical conditioning

Ivan Pavlov

neutral stimulus

unconditioned stimulus

unconditioned response

conditioned stimulus

conditioned response

acquisition

extinction

spontaneous recovery

stimulus generalization

stimulus discrimination

second-order / higher-order conditioning

John B. Watson & Rosalie Rayner

"Little Albert" study

aversive conditioning

learned taste aversion

biological preparedness

operant conditioning

Edward Thorndike

Law of Effect

instrumental learning

B. F. Skinner

positive reinforcement

negative reinforcement

primary reinforcer

secondary reinforcer

positive punishment

negative punishment / omission training

operant box / "Skinner box"

chaining

shaping

continuous reinforcement

intermittent reinforcement

schedules of reinforcement

fixed-ratio schedule

variable-ratio schedule

fixed-interval schedule

variable-interval schedule

superstition

David Premack / Premack Principle

Keller & Marian Breland

instinctual drift

Rescorla-Wagner Model / Contingency Model

observational learning

Albert Bandura

"Bobo doll" study

modeling

vicarious reinforcement

latent learning

Edward Tolman

cognitive map

abstract learning

Wolfgang Köhler

insight learning

Memory – Key Terms

encoding

storage

retrieval

3-box model

sensory memory

George Sperling

iconic memory

echoic memory

selective attention

short-term memory

George Miller

the "magical number 7"

organizational encoding

chunking

rehearsal

working memory

long-term memory

declarative / explicit memory

episodic memory

semantic memory

non-declarative / implicit memory

procedural memory

Daniel Schacter

transience

Hermann Ebbinghaus

forgetting curve

absentmindedness

blocking

tip-of-the-tongue experience

misattribution

source memory

false recognition

cryptomnesia

suggestibility

Elizabeth Loftus

reconstructive memory

bias

consistency bias

egocentric bias

persistence

flash-bulb memory

state-dependent memory

hippocampus

anterograde amnesia

retrograde amnesia

patient H.M.

long-term potentiation (LTP)

NMDA

serial position effect

primacy

recency

testing effect

distributed review

massed practice

spaced-repetition software (SRS)

overlearning

levels of processing

self-referential effect

retrieval cue

spreading activation

Method of Loci / Roman Room / Journey Method

Link / Keyword Method

Language and Cognition – Key Terms

B.F. Skinner

Noam Chomsky

language acquisition device (LAD)

linguistics

phonemes

morphemes

phonological rules

accent

syntactical rules

fast-mapping

telegraphic speech

overgeneralization / overregularization

The Wug Test

critical period

genetic dysphasia

interactionist approach

linguistic relativity hypothesis / Whorf-Sapir hypothesis

concepts and categories

prototype

exemplar theory

mental set

functional fixedness

convergent thinking

divergent thinking

overconfidence

illusory superiority / Wobegon effect

belief bias

belief perseverance

algorithm

heuristic

Amos Tversky & Daniel Kahneman

availability heuristic

representativeness heuristic

framing effect

sunk-cost fallacy

recognition heuristic

States of Consciousness – Key Terms

René Descartes

mind-body problem

Cartesian Theater

philosophical zombie

problem of other minds

Thomas Nagel

minimal consciousness

self-consciousness

mark test

"hard problem" of consciousness

unity

intentionality

selectivity

transience

cocktail-party phenomenon

dichotic listening task

selective attention

change blindness

inattentional blindness

thought suppression

dual-processing theory

System 1

System 2

priming

mere-exposure effect

circadian rhythm

zeitgeber

suprachiasmatic nucleus

pineal gland

melatonin

sleep cycle

EEG (electroencephalogram)

alpha waves

NREM stage 1

theta waves

hypnagogic imagery

hypnic jerk

NREM stage 2

sleep spindle

K-complex

NREM stage 3

delta waves

slow-wave Sleep

REM

paradoxical sleep

sleep deprivation (chronic, acute)

insomnia

sleep apnea

sleepwalking / somnambulism

night terrors

REM behavior disorder

narcolepsy

cataplexy

polyphasic sleep

Sigmund Freud

manifest content

latent content

dream interpretation

activation-synthesis hypothesis

information processing theory

memory consolidation

lucid dreaming

agonist

antagonist

homeostasis

neuroadaptation

tolerance

dependency

withdrawal

psychological addiction

stimulant

depressant

narcotic

opiates

hallucinogen

hypnosis

hypnotic suggestibility

analgesia

post-hypnotic amnesia

role theory of hypnosis

dissociation theory of hypnosis

focused attention meditation

mantra

mindfulness meditation

relaxation response

References and Recommended Reading

In preparing this series, I read thousands of pages from several editions of psychology textbooks, student guides, teacher resources, and online materials, in addition to completing coursework, listening to podcasts, and reading journal articles to better understand and explain the concepts presented here. This is not an academic research publication and to keep it in a student-friendly format that is easy to read, I decided not to create extensive footnoting or referencing in the text itself. That said, the following have been excellent sources of information, and I am indebted to all of the authors below for their clarity, insight, and information. I have listed specific journal articles for all individual studies mentioned in this text, as well as other recommended reading for students interested in exploring subjects in more detail.

General resources for all chapters

Gleitman, H., Gross, J., & Reisberg, D. (2011) Psychology (8th ed.) New York, NY: W.W. Norton & Company, Inc.

Myers, D. (2010). *Myers' Psychology for AP* (1st ed.). New York, NY: Worth.

Myers, D. (2013). Psychology (10th ed.). New York, NY: Worth.

Schacter, D.L., Gilbert, D.T., & Wegner, D.M. (2009) *Psychology.* New York, NY: Worth.

Spielman, R.M., Dumper, K., Jenkins, W., Lacombe, A., Lovett, M. & Perlmutter, M. (2014). *Psychology.* Houston, TX: OpenStax. Available at: https://openstaxcollege.org/textbooks/psychology

Weseley, A., & McEntarffer, R. (2010). *AP® Psychology* (4th ed.). Hauppauge, N.Y.: Barron's Educational Series.

Chapter 1

Bandura, A., Ross, D., & Ross, S. (1961). Transmission Of Aggression Through Imitation Of Aggressive Models. *The Journal of Abnormal and Social Psychology,* 575-582.

Bandura, A., Ross, D., & Ross, S. (1963). Imitation Of Film-mediated Aggressive Models. *The Journal of Abnormal and Social Psychology,* 3-11.

Bhatt, R., Wasserman, E., Reynolds, W., & Knauss, K. (1998). Conceptual behavior in pigeons: Categorization of both familiar and novel examples from four classes of natural and artificial stimuli. *Journal of Experimental Psychology: Animal Behavior Processes,* 219-234.

Breland, K., & Breland, M. (1961). The Misbehavior Of Organisms. *American Psychologist,* 681-684.

Garcia J., Kimeldorf D., & Koelling R. (1955) Conditioned aversion to saccharin resulting from exposure to gamma radiation. *Science,* 122(3160): 157-8.

Garcia, J., & Koelling, R. (1966) Relation of cue to consequence in avoidance learning. *Psychonomic Science, 4,* 123-124.

Premack, D. (1959). Toward empirical behavior laws: I. Positive reinforcement. *Psych Rev., 66,* 219-233

Skinner, B. (1947). 'Superstition' In The Pigeon. *Journal of Experimental Psychology,* 168-172.

Tolman, E. C., & Honzik, C. H. (1930). Introduction and removal of reward, and maze performance in rats. *University of California Publications in Psychology*.

Tolman, E. C., Ritchie, B. F., & Kalish, D. (1946). Studies in spatial learning. I. Orientation and the short-cut. *Journal of Experimental Psychology, 36,* 13-24.

Tolman, E. C. (1948). Cognitive maps in rats and men. *Psychological review*, 55(4), 189.

Watanabe, S., Sakamoto, J., & Wakita, M. (1995) Pigeon's discrimination of paintings by Monet and Picasso, *Journal of the Experimental Analysis of Behavior,* 63, pp. 165–174

Watson, J., & Rayner, R. (1920). Conditioned Emotional Reactions. *Journal of Experimental Psychology, 3,* 1-14.

Recommended Reading:

Burgess, A. (1986). *A Clockwork Orange*. New York: Norton.

Skinner, B. (1976). *Walden Two*. New York: Macmillan.

Chapter 2

Anderson, J. (1983). A Spreading Activation Theory Of Memory. *Journal of Verbal Learning and Verbal Behavior,* 261-295.

Atkinson, R. & Shiffrin, R. (1968). Human memory: A proposed system and its control processes. In Spence, K.W.; Spence, J.T. *The psychology of learning and motivation (Volume 2)*. New York: Academic Press. pp. 89–195.

Craik, F., & Lockhart, R. (1972) Levels of Processing: A Framework for Memory Research. *Journal of Verbal Learning and Verbal Behavior* 11: 671-684.

Loftus, E., & Pickrell J. (1995). The formation of false memories. *Psychiatric Annals* 25: 720–725.

Loftus, E., & Palmer, J. (1974). Reconstruction of automobile destruction: An example of the interaction between language and memory. *Journal of Verbal Learning and Verbal Behavior,* 585-589.

Miller, G. (1956). The Magical Number Seven, Plus Or Minus Two: Some Limits On Our Capacity For Processing Information. *Psychological Review,* 81-97.

Morris, R., Anderson, E., Lynch, G., & Baudry, M. (1986). Selective Impairment Of Learning And Blockade Of Long-term Potentiation By An N-methyl-D-aspartate Receptor Antagonist, AP5. *Nature,* 774-776.

Paivio, A (1969). Mental Imagery in associative learning and memory. *Psychological Review,* 76(3), 241-263.

Scoville, W., & Milner, B. (1957). Loss of recent memory after bilateral hippocampal lesions. *Journal of Neurology, Neurosurgery and Psychiatry* 20 (1): 11–21.

Sperling G. (1960) The information available in brief visual presentations. *Psychological Monogr.* 74:1-29.

Tulving, E. (1966) Subjective Organization and Effects of Repetition in Multi-Trial Free-Recall Learning. *Journal of Verbal Learning and Verbal Behavior*, Volume 5.

Recommended Reading:

Foer, J. (2011). *Moonwalking with Einstein: The art and science of remembering everything*. New York: Penguin Press.

O'Brien, D. (1993). *How to Develop a Perfect Memory*. London: Pavilion.

Schacter, D. (2001). *The Seven Sins of Memory: How the mind forgets and remembers*. Boston: Houghton Mifflin.

Wearing, Deborah (2005) The man who keeps falling in love with his wife. Available at: http://www.telegraph.co.uk/news/health/3313452/The-man-who-keeps-falling-in-love-with-his-wife.html

Chapter 3

Adams, P., & Adams, J. (1960). Confidence in the recognition and reproduction of words difficult to spell. *The American journal of psychology* 73: 544–552.

Berko, Jean (1958). The Child's Learning of English Morphology. *Word*: 150–177.

Chomsky, N. (1959). A Review of Skinner's Verbal Behavior. *Language* 35 (1): 26–58.

Evans, J. St. B.T., Barston, J.L., & Pollard, P. (1983). On the conflict between logic and belief in syllogistic reasoning. *Memory and Cognition* 11: 295–306.

Goldstein, D., & Gigerenzer, G. (2002). Models Of Ecological Rationality: The Recognition Heuristic. *Psychological Review,* 75-90.

Johnson, E., & Goldstein, D. (2003) Do Defaults Save Lives? *Science*, Vol. 302, pp. 1338-1339.

Kahneman, D., & Tversky, A. (1979). Prospect theory: An analysis of decisions under risk. *Econometrica* 47 (2): 263–291.

Lord, C., Lepper, M., & Preston, E. (1984). Considering the opposite: A corrective strategy for social judgment. *Journal of Personality and Social Psychology*, 47, 1231-1243.

Maslow, A. (1966). *The psychology of science; a reconnaissance,.* New York: Harper & Row. p.15.

Pilkington, K. (Presenter) (2010) China [Television series episode]. In *An Idiot Abroad* British Sky Broadcasting.

Ramírez-Esparza, N., Gosling, S. D., Benet-Martínez, V., Potter, J., & Pennebaker, J. W. (2006). Do bilinguals have two personalities? A special case of cultural frame switching. *Journal of Research in Personality*, 40, 99-120.

Ross, L., Lepper, M., & Hubbard, M. (1975). Perseverance In Self-perception And Social Perception: Biased Attributional Processes In The Debriefing Paradigm. *Journal of Personality and Social Psychology,* 880-892.

Ross, M., Xun, W., & Wilson, A. (2002). Language And The Bicultural Self. *Personality and Social Psychology Bulletin,* 1040-1050.

Skinner, B. (1957). *Verbal behavior.* New York: Appleton-Century-Crofts.

Tversky, A., & Kahneman, D. (1973). Availability: A heuristic for judging frequency and probability. *Cognitive Psychology* 5 (2): 207–232.

Tversky, A., & Kahneman, D. (1974). Judgment under uncertainty: Heuristics and biases. *Science* 185 (4157): 1124–1131.

Tversky, A., & Kahneman, D. (1981). The framing of decisions and the psychology of choice. *Science* 211 (4481): 453–458.

Recommended Reading:

Ariely, D. (2010). *Predictably irrational: The hidden forces that shape our decisions.* New York: Harper Perennial.

Pinker, S. (2007). *The Stuff of Thought: Language as a window into human nature.* New York: Viking.

Kahneman, D. (2011). *Thinking, Fast and Slow.* New York: Farrar, Straus and Giroux.

Chapter 4

Drowsy Driving Facts and Stats from the National Sleep Foundation and the National Highway Traffic Safety Administration. Retrieved February 7, 2015, from http://drowsydriving.org/about/facts-and-stats/

Bargh, J., Chen, M., & L. Burrows. (1996). Automaticity of social behavior: Direct effects of trait construct and stereotype activation on action. *Journal of Personality and Social Psychology*, 71, 230-244

Cherry, E. (1953). Some Experiments On The Recognition Of Speech, With One And With Two Ears. *The Journal of the Acoustical Society of America,* 975-975.

Green, J.P., & Lynn, S.J. (2005). Hypnosis vs. relaxation: Accuracy and confidence in dating international news events. *Applied Cognitive Psychology*, 19, 679- 691.

Heider, F, & Simmel, M. (1944). An experimental study of apparent behavior. *American Journal of Psychology, 57,* 243–259.

Hobson, J. A., & McCarley, R. (1977). The Brain as A Dream State Generator: An Activation-Synthesis Hypothesis of the Dream Process. *The American Journal of Psychiatry* 134 (12): 1335–48.

Nagel, T. (1974). What Is It Like to Be a Bat? *The Philosophical Review,* 435-450.

Ricard, M., Lutz, A., & Davidson, R.J. (2014) Mind of the Meditator. *Scientific American, 311(5),* 38-45

Simons D., & Chabris C. (1999) Gorillas in our midst: sustained inattentional blindness for dynamic events. *Perception* 28(9), 1059 – 1074

Simons, D., & Levin, D. (1998), Failure to detect changes to people during a real-world interaction, *Psychonomic Bulletin and Review* 5 (4): 644–649

Stampi, C. (1989) Polyphasic sleep strategies improve prolonged sustained performance: A field study on 99 sailors. *Work & Stress, 3, 1*, 41-55.

Van Gulick, R. (2014) Consciousness. *The Stanford Encyclopedia of Philosophy* (Spring 2014 Edition), Edward N. Zalta (ed.), URL = <http://plato.stanford.edu/archives/spr2014/entries/consciousness/>.

Wamsley, E., Tucker, M., Payne, J., Benavides, J., & Stickgold, R. (2010). Dreaming Of A Learning Task Is Associated With Enhanced Sleep-Dependent Memory Consolidation. *Current Biology,* 850-855.

Wegner, D. M., Schneider, D. J., Carter, S., & White, T. (1987). Paradoxical effects of thought suppression. *Journal of Personality and Social Psychology, 53,* 5-13.

Zeidan, F., Grant, J., Brown, C., Mchaffie, J., & Coghill, R. (2012). Mindfulness meditation-related pain relief: Evidence for unique brain mechanisms in the regulation of pain. *Neuroscience Letters,* 165-173.

Recommended Reading:

Benson, H. (1975). *The Relaxation Response.* New York: Morrow.

Freud, S., & Crick, J. (1999). *The Interpretation of Dreams.* Oxford: Oxford University Press.

LaBerge, S., & Rheingold, H. (1990). *Exploring the World of Lucid Dreaming.* New York: Ballantine Books.

Sacks, O. (2012). *Hallucinations.* New York: Alfred A. Knopf.

Wegner, D. (2002). *The Illusion of Conscious Will.* Cambridge, Mass.: MIT Press.

Zinn, J. (2004). *Wherever You Go, There You Are.* London: Piatkus.

About the Author

Michael Corayer earned his Bachelor's degree in Psychology from Harvard in 2006. Michael taught Advanced Placement and International Baccalaureate Psychology courses at an international school in Shanghai, China from 2008 until 2015. He also writes for www.psychexamreview.com, a resource for students of psychology.

37461433R00071

Made in the USA
Middletown, DE
28 November 2016